The
SECOND
Coming of
CHRIST

The

SECOND
Coming of
CHRIST

Aimee
Semple McPherson

WHITAKER
HOUSE

All Scripture quotations are taken from
the King James Version of the Holy Bible.

Boldface type in the Scripture quotations indicates the author's emphasis.

The Second Coming of Christ

ISBN: 978-1-62911-016-5
eBook ISBN: 978-1-62911-040-0
Printed in the United States of America
© 1920, 2014 by Whitaker House

Whitaker House
1030 Hunt Valley Circle
New Kensington, PA 15068
www.whitakerhouse.com

Library of Congress Cataloging-in-Publication Data (Pending)

1 2 3 4 5 6 7 8 9 10 11 **W** 21 20 19 18 17 16 15 14

CONTENTS

PREFACE

Since the blessed Lord so tenderly called this writer unto Himself, washed her heart in His blessed blood, baptized her with the Holy Spirit, called her from a home on a Canadian farm to preach the gospel, and began to open the Word before her adoring eyes, the second coming of Jesus Christ has ever been, above all things, the dearest to her heart.

Surely, the coming of the Master is drawing near. It behooves us, therefore, as His Spirit-filled children, to bear this blessed message of warning and hope without delay to the sleeping world about us.

"Prepare ye the way of the Lord, make his paths straight" (Mark 1:3) was the commission of John the Baptist. His first advent.

Lift up thy voice in the wilderness of sin and worldliness and cry, *"Prepare ye the way of the Lord.'* Jesus is coming; get ready to meet Him; watch, for He is near, even at the door" is the message of the awakening church today.

In these last days, the Lord is pouring out His Spirit upon all flesh. The time for a mighty revival is upon us. Thousands are being saved and sealed with the Spirit in this closing hour, so that the reaper is made to overtake the plower. Fields stand ripe for the harvest on every hand, and what is to be done must be done quickly.

To this end, this book is lovingly and prayerfully dedicated, not only to those who love His appearing, but also to those in slumber who have not yet heard the call. Oh, that through these pages they might hear the awakening cry of the Holy Spirit, "*Behold, the bridegroom cometh; go ye out to meet him*" (Matthew 25:6), and that the writer and the reader may both rise to meet Him when He shall appear in the clouds of glory! God grant that this "*blessed hope*" (Titus 2:13) may be implanted in every heart. For if any man "*hath this hope in him purifieth himself, even as [Christ] is pure*" (1 John 3:3), then "*when he shall appear, we shall be like him; for we shall see him as he is*" (verse 2).

—*Aimee Semple McPherson*

1

IS HE COMING?

That the Lord Jesus Christ is coming back to this earth someday, no honest believer in the Word of God can doubt. Most emphatically and unmistakably does the sacred page declare it.

In the Old Testament, there are twenty times as many references to the second coming of Christ as to His first coming; that is, twenty times as many references to His coming as a crowned King, seated upon the throne of David, ruling with a rod of iron, bringing victory and glory unto Jerusalem, and peace upon earth as to His coming—a meek and lowly Jesus, wounded for our transgressions, bruised for our iniquities, and bleeding as a slain Lamb upon the cursed tree. There are twenty times as many references to His coming with a *crown*, honored and worshiped by all the ends of the earth, as to His coming with a *cross*, and being wounded in the house of His friends.

Thus it was that the Jews, who had been looking for a mighty king, failed to recognize the lowly Nazarene, and still refuse to recognize Him even to this day. And yet, the cross must ever precede the crown. If you don't bear the cross, you can't wear the crown. He came with the cross, fulfilling the prophecy of Isaiah 53; and now He is coming with a crown, the Messiah and King of Isaiah 9:7 and of Jeremiah 3:17. Not only did He come to the earth once—*"Christ was once offered to bear the sins of many"* (Hebrews 9:28)—but *"unto them that look for him shall he appear the second time"* (verse 28).

The New Testament declares His coming. In the 260 chapters of the New Testament, the second coming of Jesus Christ is definitely referred to 318 times. Someone has estimated that one out of every thirty verses is devoted to this great and glorious theme.

The epistles of Paul, while referring to water baptism only thirteen times, refer to the second coming fifty times. This is the *"blessed hope"* (Titus 2:13) with which the members of the church body are told to comfort one another.

Every time you repeat the Lord's Prayer, you are praying for Christ's return: *"Thy kingdom come. Thy will be done in earth, as it is in heaven"* (Matthew 6:10). How can there be a kingdom without a King, or His righteous reign be established upon the earth till Christ returns to rout the hosts of darkness, cast down satanic rule, and wield His own dear scepter over the lands?

The last prayer in the Bible is a great heart-throbbing cry for His return: *"Even so, come, Lord Jesus"* (Revelation 22:20). And the answer still rings from heaven: *"Behold, I come quickly; and my reward is with me"* (verse 12).

Jesus Himself promised that He would return, saying, *"If I go and prepare a place for you, I will come again"* (John 14:3). What could be plainer than this statement of our Lord? "If I go away, I will come again."

Did He go away? Yes. Acts 1:9 is careful to give us a clear description of our Lord's departure from this earth: *"When he had spoken these things, while they beheld, he was taken up; and a cloud received him out of their sight."*

"If I go." Yes, there He goes, slowly, majestically, the literal, visible Jesus is ascending into the heavens. Higher, higher He rises, up and up till the clouds receive Him out of the disciples' sight. And there they stand, watching Him go.

"Ah, there He goes, my beautiful Master" the voice of John the Beloved must have mourned. "When will I ever rest my head upon His loving breast again?"

"Lord, Lord, when shall I again gaze into Your precious face, sit at Your feet, and hear Your tender voice?" Mary the sister of Martha must have sobbed.

"Gone, gone! My Lord is gone! But what was that He said? *'If I go…I will come again.'* He has surely gone away, but will He come again?"

The angels also testify. Suddenly, two men in white apparel stood by them, saying, *"Ye men of Galilee, why stand ye gazing up into heaven? this same Jesus, which is taken up from you into heaven, shall so come in like manner as ye have seen him go into heaven"* (Acts 1:11).

"This same Jesus" shall return. Not some mythical, intangible, invisible Spirit, but *this same Jesus*—the Jesus who ate bread and fish and honey before their eyes after His resurrection, the Christ who said, *"Behold my hands and my feet, that it is I myself: handle me, and see"* (Luke 24:39).

Oh, glory to His dear name! Small wonder that they returned to Jerusalem with joy. Why, the message of our Lord's second coming is the most joyful message that could be borne to the heart of a believer, by man or by angel. It spells joy to the children of light, for then, the sun will be risen; and woes to the children of darkness, for sin and night will then be conquered and banished forever.

The apostle Paul bears witness to His coming in 1 Thessalonians 4:16–17, saying,

> For the Lord himself shall descend from heaven with a shout, with the voice of the archangel, and with the trump of God: and the dead in Christ shall rise first: then we which are alive and remain shall be caught up together with them in the clouds, to meet the Lord in the air: and so shall we ever be with the Lord.

The Holy Spirit declares His coming is near, ringing the glorious words through waiting hearts, "Jesus is coming soon; get ready!"

The signs of the times, when compared with Bible prophecy, declare that His coming is near. Unbelievers may scoff at the thought of His personal and literal return for His waiting church, as the people of Noah's day scoffed at the declaration of the coming flood. But as sure as the flood came and caught faithful Noah up on its heaving bosom, leaving the sinful and unbelieving to be buried beneath the rising waves, so certainly will Christ, the blessed Bridegroom of the church, return to take His bride away, leaving the foolish virgins and the unprepared to be covered by the waves of tribulation.

Jesus is coming! What if He should come tonight? Does your heart leap exultantly at the thought? Are you ready to meet Him, washed in His precious blood, filled with His Holy Spirit? If not, seek Him today; there is no time to lose. Buy oil, that your lamps and vessels may be filled; then when the door of translation is opened in the skies, you will go into the marriage of the Lamb.

2

HOW IS HE COMING?

So glorious and inspiring is the theme of Christ's second coming, so filled with hope and life and comfort, that it makes the cords of the waiting heart vibrate as a harp swept by the celestial melodies of "That Blessed Hope."

Coming again! Oh hallelujah! That tender, merciful, understanding Jesus. That dear Son of God who took the little children in His arms and blessed them; who healed the sick and raised the dead and cleansed the leper; who fed the hungry, forgave the sinner, and bound up the brokenhearted. That precious Lamb of Calvary, whose bleeding wounds were opened wide. That mighty resurrected crowned King of heaven and earth. That coming Bridegroom of the church. Oh bless His precious name! He's coming back again.

He's coming back in power and glory, surrounded by an innumerable company of angels, robed in His kingly garments, with sandals upon His feet and a scepter in His hand. Coming—but here! We are to study God's Word today and seek the answer to the question *"How* is He coming?"

No truth is more firmly established on biblical foundation, no truth more emphasized in the Word, than the second coming of Jesus. All must admit that according to the Word of God, Jesus Christ has promised to come back to this earth—sometime, somehow. As to the manner of His coming, there are many theories.

First, there are those who believe that the coming of the Lord was spiritually fulfilled on the day of Pentecost. They declare that He who ascended with a resurrected body before the eyes of His disciples returned after ten days in Spirit form to comfort, guide, and endue his little ones with power for service in the preaching of the gospel.

True, there was great power and a real person of the Trinity that descended upon and entered into them upon that day. This person, however, was not the Lord Jesus Christ, but the Holy Spirit—the third person in the Trinity—of whom He had spoken, saying,

> *And I will pray the Father, and he shall give you another Comforter.* (John 14:16)

> *It is expedient for you that I go away: for if I go not away, the Comforter will not come unto you; but if I depart, I will send him unto you.* (John 16:7)

> *For he shall not speak of himself; but whatsoever he shall hear, that shall he speak.* (verse 13)

> *He shall glorify me: for he shall receive of mine, and shall show it unto you.* (verse 14)

Plainly, Christ is not speaking of Himself but of another, namely, the Holy Spirit, the third person in the Godhead. Let us not confuse the office work of the Spirit with that of the Son, for while the Spirit was being poured out upon the waiting church, Christ was at the right hand of the Father in glory, where Stephen saw him some time later.

There are those who believe that the destruction of Jerusalem in A.D. 70 was the second coming of the Lord. But a moment's thought and honest study of the Scriptures disproves the truth of such a statement to the heart of the believer. His coming is to be marked not by the destruction of Jerusalem but by its restoration. The Jews who have been torn and driven away will be brought again unto their own land. After their deception and tribulation through the Antichrist, they will see the Lord coming in the clouds of heaven—their Messiah, the Prince of Peace—with healing in His wings.

Then, too, the signs predicted to accompany the second advent of the Lord from heaven were not fulfilled during the destruction of Jerusalem. The graves were not opened for *"the dead in Christ* [to] *rise"* (1 Thessalonians 4:16), neither were the living saints *"caught up together…to meet the Lord in the air"* (verse 17). The gospel had not yet been preached unto the ends of the earth. This was a time of seed sowing, not a time to harvest the ripened grain.

There are others who declare that the coming of the Lord means nothing more or less than *conversion*—the coming of the Lord into the sinner's heart.

At conversion, however, the sinner comes to the Lord, not the Lord to the sinner. The convicted soul is led to the "fountain filled with blood" by the Holy Spirit, who makes plain unto him the finished work of Calvary, and who bears witness with His spirit that the lost soul is a child of God. Although there is a definite and blessed way in which Christ is enthroned in the hearts of His people at regeneration, it would not be the definite second coming, for which the apostle looked forward to with unutterable yearning and referred to throughout the years as "that blessed hope, the second coming of the Lord Jesus Christ." (See Titus 2:13.) His coming will be attended by opening graves, resurrected saints, and stupendous power and glory.

There are those who maintain that the coming of the Lord takes place at death. They declare that there will be no coming other than that which everyone experiences when he passes out of his body *"to be present with the Lord"* (2 Corinthians 5:8).

But here again, the life goes to Christ instead of Christ coming to the life. If death were the coming of the Lord, Christ would need to come to this earth many, many times each day. We are told that at every tick of the clock, some soul passes into eternity. Jesus would not be in glory to fulfill His high priestly duties at the right hand of the Father, where He continually makes intercession for the saints. No, bless the Lord, the coming of the Lord will not mean death but life—not a going down into the grave but a coming out of it in a resurrection bright and fair.

There is still another class who believe that the spreading of the gospel of Jesus Christ into the remotest corners of heathendom is the coming of the Lord. A moment's reflection upon this subject, however, convinces us that this, too, is a mistaken thought. His coming is to be sudden. He is to appear *"in the twinkling of an eye"* (1 Corinthians 15:52), and with the rapidity with which the light rings flash across the heavens from the east unto the west. *"There shall be two men in one bed; the one shall be taken, and the other shall be left"* (Luke 17:34). Whereas the sending forth of missionaries and the propagation of the gospel takes centuries, and is, all must admit, a slow and tedious process.

If, therefore, none of these events are the coming of Christ, what is the solution of the question How is He coming?

The best and only way to determine this is to ascertain what the Scriptures say. How does God's Word say He is coming?

Let us turn again to the first chapter of Acts, with its marvelous and graphic description of Christ's ascension and the succeeding events. Jesus Christ, in bodily form, was resurrected from the grave and walked the earth for forty days. During this time, He visibly appeared to more than five hundred people. (See 1 Corinthians 15:6.) His precious blood had been shed on Calvary, but His body of flesh and bones, which they had laid in the tomb, had been resurrected.

So real and tangible was this body that, to doubting Thomas, Jesus said, *"Reach hither thy finger, and behold my hands; and reach hither thy hand, and thrust it into my side"* (John 20:27). This resurrected Lord had built a fire upon the shore, broiled fish and bread upon the coals, and eaten before their eyes. In this chapter, He stands forth in their midst giving a last word of instruction and exhortation.

> *When he had spoken these things, while they beheld, he was taken up; and a cloud received him out of their sight. And while they looked stedfastly toward heaven as he went up, behold, two men stood by them in white apparel; which also said, Ye men of Galilee, why stand ye gazing up into heaven? this same Jesus, which is taken up from you into heaven, shall so come in like manner as ye have seen him go into heaven.*
> (Acts 1:9–11)

The Same Visible, Tangible Jesus

Here, we are plainly told how He is coming. *"This same Jesus"*—with the same resurrected body that you now behold, the same pierced feet and hands, and the same tender heart—which is taken up from you into heaven, shall so come in like manner as you have seen Him go.

He went up slowly and visibly, a majestic, literal, resurrected Jesus, into the clouds of heaven. His disciples stood and watched Him go, up and up, until the clouds hid His dear form from view. He will return *"in like manner"*—i.e., in the clouds of heaven. Made visible to His waiting children, He will descend from heaven, coming in power, bringing with Him an innumerable company of angels, to take His loved ones home.

In the Clouds

Behold, he cometh with clouds. (Revelation 1:7)

The Lord himself shall descend from heaven with a shout, with the voice of the archangel, and with the trump of God: and the dead in Christ shall rise first: then we which are alive and remain shall be caught up together with them in the clouds, to meet the Lord in the air: and so shall we ever be with the Lord. (1 Thessalonians 4:16–17)

Here is a real event, described so plainly and unmistakably in God's Word that it cannot be explained away, or mean anything else than exactly what it says. This is a definite event, happening at a definite time. The words we have quoted can mean but one thing: that these same heavens of blue, with their fleecy clouds, are to be parted wide by the returning of the Son of God. One of these days, they will light up with His glory as He descends out of heaven from God.

With a Shout

We are told that He is coming *"with a shout"* (1 Thessalonians 4:16). Oh, dear reader, does not your whole being thrill and your heart beat faster at the words *"The Lord himself shall descend from heaven with a shout, with the voice of the archangel, and with the trump of God"*?

What a shout, what a voice. What a trumpet that will be for those with listening ears! Oh, are you listening for that sound—listening in the busy, roaring streets; listening in the silence of the night; keeping your ears clean and closed to the gossip and foolish jesting all about you; listening, waiting, ready for that sound?

He *"shall descend from heaven with a shout."* Oh, glorious message that fills the soul with joy and the eyes with happy tears! That mighty *"voice of the archangel,"* that *"trump of God,"* will cause the very earth to vibrate and will penetrate the deepest graves in land or sea.

There is no grave too far away in Africa's burning sand or Greenland's icy mountains that His voice will not reach and penetrate; no stone or mausoleum too solid that His voice will not penetrate. It will be heard in every quarter of the earth where there abides a waiting, ready heart.

If this is such a great shout, will the sinful masses of earth also hear it and understand its import?

In all probability, they will hear a sound of some sort, but it is doubtful that they will recognize it as the voice of the Lord. When Jesus was baptized by John in the Jordan River, God spoke from heaven, saying, *"This is my beloved Son, in whom I am well pleased"* (Matthew 3:17). The people of that day did not recognize the voice of God; however, many thought that it had thundered; others thought an angel had spoken. When Jesus appeared and spoke to Saul on the road to Damascus, the voice, while intelligible to Saul, was not understood by those who accompanied him. It would not be surprising, therefore, if the same thing occurred at Christ's second coming.

Perhaps, on that day, some godly little servant girl will be waiting upon the table of her rich and fashionable mistress. The afternoon card games over, dinner is being served faultlessly. Sparkling witticisms are being exchanged over the snowy linen, with its shining silver and fragrant blossoms.

The maid (let's call her Miss Faithful) is obediently serving the soup and oysters, but her heart is far above all the frivolity that surrounds her. She is thinking of Christ's coming, and of another table—the marriage supper of the Lamb—where she will be a guest and where the angels will serve the tables.

Suddenly, a loud and most peculiarly indefinable sound is heard from above, which causes the very window panes to rattle and the delicate china to tinkle.

"Mercy! What was that?" asks someone, nervously.

"Sounded to me like thunder," replies another, glancing through the window. "The sky has been a little cloudy this afternoon. I guess we may have a little shower. Nothing to be alarmed about, I'm sure."

"Oh, dear, thunderstorms and lightning make me so nervous," trembles the worldly, unprepared mistress, "but I guess this will pass over." Her hand trembles visibly as she sounds the table chime for Miss Faithful.

The moments pass, and yet, no Miss Faithful appears with the roast fowl and vegetables. What can be keeping the girl?

The mistress rings again and yet, no servant. She grows embarrassed and rings again. This time, the puzzled woman excuses herself and goes to the kitchen door. Never before has the obedient, respectful servant neglected her duty in this manner.

"Miss Faithful! where are you?"

No reply.

"Cook, where are you, and do you know anything about Miss Faithful?"

Still no reply.

They are nowhere to be found; there is the dinner on the tray, ready to be served; there is the pan that has just boiled dry on the stove, beginning to burn. On the window seat, there is an open Bible, marked at 1 Thessalonians 4:16.

Impatiently, she touches the button for the chauffeur. "Perkins, have you seen Miss Faithful or the cook anywhere?"

"No, ma'am, I saw them last just before they began to prepare dinner. While you were playing card games, they were having a little prayer meeting here in the kitchen, and Miss Faithful was reading 'the Book' over there."

How very strange! The mistress finally serves the dinner herself and engages new servants the following day. The subject of conversation at the dinner turns to the large number of unexplained disappearances that fill newspapers, and the episode is dropped. To the hearts of the sinful worldlings, it was nothing but the sound of thunder. To Miss Faithful and the Christian cook, it was the voice of the Lord.

Suddenly

The coming of the Lord will take place in an instant, and without warning:

> But of that day and hour knoweth no man, no, not the angels of heaven, but my Father only. But as the days of Noe were, so shall also the coming of the Son of man be. For as in the days that were before the flood they were eating and drinking, marrying and giving in marriage, until the day that Noe entered into the ark, and knew not until the flood came, and took them

all away; so shall also the coming of the Son of man be.
(Matthew 24:36–39)

There will be no time to prepare in that moment. Those who are ready will be caught up with Him in the air; but those who are unprepared will be left behind. Then shall two be in the field; the one shall be taken, and the other left. In that sudden moment, one part of the globe will be shrouded in darkness, and its inhabitants asleep in their beds. Somewhere it is early morn, and women are grinding their morning meal; while still in another quarter of the sphere, it is broad daylight, and the harvesters are toiling in the field.

The suddenness of His coming is again described in the parable of the ten virgins:

> *They that were ready went in with him to the marriage: and the door was shut.…Watch therefore, for ye know neither the day nor the hour wherein the Son of man cometh.*
> (Matthew 25:10, 13)

The last words of Christ recorded in the Bible concern the suddenness of His coming: *"Surely I come quickly"* (Revelation 22:20). And the last recorded cry of the church bride is embodied in the answering words of John the Beloved: *"Amen. Even so, come, Lord Jesus"* (Revelation 22:20).

Jesus is speaking to your heart even now, saying, "Behold, I come quickly." Oh, can you lift up your face to the clouds of heaven and, with clean hands and a pure heart, cry with joy, "Amen, even so, come, Lord Jesus"? If not, there is no time to lose. Today is the day of preparation; tomorrow may be too late.

As a Thief in the Night

The Word of God tells us that at His second coming, Christ will come *"as a thief in the night"* (1 Thessalonians 5:2).

A thief comes to the home at an hour when least expected; and the occupants of the home are not notified as to the hour of his arrival.

A thief comes with a definite object in view. When it is accomplished, he quickly and quietly takes his departure, carrying with him that for which he had come.

A thief does not seek the wooden furniture or the carpets. He comes for the gold, the silver, and the precious stones.

And, indeed, the richest treasure the earth holds today is the redeemed, blood-washed, spirit-filled believers who await the coming of Jesus Christ. All else God considers as wood, hay, and stubble. He is coming for the *gold*, tried in the furnace of affliction; the *silver* of atonement, wrought out in yielded lives; the *precious stones* that adorn the soulwinner's crown, stones mined from the depths, cut and polished by the Master's hands into jeweled graces that adorn the Christian life.

Many homes will be left desolate. The godly mother, the Spirit-filled husband, and the precious children all have been caught out and up. To the mourners who refuse to believe or prepare, Christ says,

> But know this, that if the goodman of the house had known in what watch the thief would come, he would have watched, and would not have suffered his house to be broken up. Therefore be ye also ready: for in such an hour as ye think not the Son of man cometh. (Matthew 24:43–44)

As a Kingly Bridegroom

Jesus our Lord is never coming back to this earth to be spit upon, bruised and beaten, ignominiously insulted, and nailed to the tree. Bless His dear name! He is coming back a mighty, triumphant King! His crown will be upon His head, and His scepter in His hand. Once has He appeared to put away sin by the sacrifice of Himself: *"Christ was once offered to bear the sins of many; and unto them that look for him shall he appear the second time without sin unto salvation"* (Hebrews 9:28).

In that day, the rainbow of peace will be under His feet, and His people shall weep no more. Storms will be over. Death and woe can never touch them more.

He is coming as a mighty victor, triumphant over death, hell, and the grave. Surely at the stately steps of His approaching feet, the stars of the morning will again break forth into singing; the hills and the mountains will flow down with praise; the sea and the caverns of the deep will lift their voices and thunder His glory; and all the earth will declare that He is the King of Kings and the Lord of Lords.

3

WHEN IS HE COMING?

Being fully persuaded by the Scriptures, both as to His coming and the manner in which He shall appear, the next great breathless question that leaps to the heart and mind is, *When* is He coming?

The stars in the heaven, the clouds of the sky, the prayers of God's people, the song of the saints, life and death, and the preaching of the gospel—everything has a new meaning! New emotions stir the waiting heart to its very depths, the most steady pulse is made to quicken, and into the eyes grown dim with care and sorrow a new light wells and shines with quenchless hope.

Jesus is coming! Those stars will tremble; those clouds will flash with His glory! Death will be swallowed up in life, and the flooding light of dawn will vanquish the pall of darkness. The patient face of the watcher in the night will be suffused with the glad eternal light of a new day. Tears will be dried forever; burdens will roll away as the unfolding curtains of the heaven reveal the face of our blessed Bridegroom.

O head once crowned with thorns, now crowned with victorious and kingly glory! O face fairer than the morning, purer than the lilies of the valley. O eyes that gaze with yearning love and pity on Your little one. Oh blessed form, clad in Your garments that smell of myrrh and aloes and cassia, when will You come forth from the ivory palaces? When, oh when, shall we gaze into the heavens and behold You coming in glorious majesty? When shall we hear Your voice, whose trumpet tones shall cause the hills to tremble, the caverns of the sea to echo, and the Christians' graves to loosen their bands?

Small wonder that after the announcement of a day of such ineffable glory, the disciples came unto their Lord privately and put to Him the question *"Tell us, when shall these things be? and what shall be the sign of thy coming, and of the end of the world?"* (Matthew 24:3).

These three questions concern three distinct events:

1. The destruction of Jerusalem and its temple, the overthrow of Jewish rule, and the dispersion of Israel.

2. The second coming of Christ for His saints, when they should be caught up to meet Him in the air for the marriage of the Lamb.

3. The end of the world (or the age), when Satan should be cast down forever, the earth cleansed by fire, and God Himself stretches forth His scepter over the new heavens and the new earth.

When is He coming? What shall be the sign of His coming? Is His coming near at hand? Is it possible for anyone to know the exact time when He will appear?

These and a score of other eager questions come trooping to the portals of the Word, beseeching answer. Let us consider

Christ's answer to these queries, for He has answered them, every one!

Before going further, let us bear in mind the fact that the second coming of Jesus Christ is divided into two parts:

1. His coming *for* His people. (See 1 Thessalonians 4:17.)
2. His coming *with* His people. (See Deuteronomy 33:2; Matthew 25:31–35.)

When Jesus comes *for* His people, His appearance is likened to a *"bright and morning star"* (Revelation 22:16). His second coming will herald the near-approaching day whose light shall never fade. This coming for His people will be followed by the bitterest tribulation the world has ever known.

When He comes *with* His people, He shall arise as *"the Sun of righteousness…with healing in his wings"* (Malachi 4:2). Satan shall be bound, the hosts of darkness conquered, and His righteous rule shall be established in the earth. (See Revelation 20:2–4.) When He comes for His people, only the waiting saints will see and meet Him in the air. When He returns, bringing His saints with Him, every eye shall see Him; weeping and consternation shall fill the hearts of those who rejected Him.

Can Anyone Know the Day or Hour?

No! Christ's Word explicitly answers this question in the negative: *"Watch therefore, for ye know neither the day nor the hour wherein the Son of man cometh"* (Matthew 25:13) and, *"Of that day and hour knoweth no man, no, not the angels of heaven, but my Father only"* (Matthew 24:36).

Though we may not know the day nor the hour, we are told that of the *"times and the seasons"* (1 Thessalonians 5:1), we need not be *"ignorant"* (1 Thessalonians 4:13).

In this respect, Jesus' second coming is remarkably similar to His first coming. The faithful few who were looking for and earnestly expecting Christ's first coming to this earth knew neither the day nor the hour. They were not in ignorance, however, as to the seasons.

Take, for instance, the magi. According to Scripture, which they earnestly searched, and the signs of the times to which they were aware, they were certain the time was at hand. Yet not until they saw the star itself did they know the day or the hour of His appearance.

The mother of Jesus, though mindful of the seasons, knew neither the day nor the hour till the time was fulfilled.

To Simeon, a man just and devout, waiting for the consolation of Israel (or the coming of the Lord), it was revealed that before he should taste death, he would see the Messiah. (See Luke 2:26.) Here again, as in the case of Anna the prophetess, is an example of those who knew the seasons but not the day or the hour.

Were the world to know definitely that the Lord would not come for five years, many would delay their preparations and say, "I still have time." But knowing that the signs predicted to precede His second coming are practically all fulfilled, and that the Holy Spirit is sending forth the last call *"Behold, the bridegroom cometh; go ye out to meet him"* (Matthew 25:6), there is every reason for haste and immediate preparation. *"Take ye heed, watch and pray: for ye know not when the time is"* (Mark 13:33).

We do know the coming of the Lord must be pre-millennial, for the righteous dead are raised up before the thousand-year reign, to sit with Christ upon His throne. (See Revelation 20:4–5.) The devil is bound before the millennium (see Revelation 20:1–5), and the Antichrist destroyed before this day. (See 2 Thessalonians 2:8.)

Signs That His Coming Is Near at Hand

There is also every reason to believe His coming to be near, even at the door. In answer to the questions of His disciples in Matthew 24, Jesus told of many signs that will precede and indicate the approach of that day; signs that were to be seen in things national, spiritual, and educational, and touch every walk and calling in life. These signs were to point like mileposts to that great event.

> *Take heed lest any man deceive you: for many shall come in my name, saying, I am Christ; and shall deceive many.*
> (Mark 13:5–6)

> *Wherefore if they shall say unto you, Behold, he is in the desert; go not forth: behold, he is in the secret chambers; believe it not. For as the lightning cometh out of the east, and shineth even unto the west; so shall also the coming of the Son of man be.* (Matthew 24:26–27)

False Christs

As we read these signs, let us check off, one by one, all that have been fulfilled. Has anyone ever had the audacity to come saying, "I am Christ?" And is it possible that so preposterous a statement would deceive many?

Yes, such impostors have come with their varied claims that they were Jesus the Christ, come to earth again. Among the number might be mentioned are Sweinfurth, Dora Beekman of Minnesota, and Mr. Herron of Detroit, Michigan, who declared himself to be "Prince Michael," supposedly fulfilling Daniel 1:11. In mentioning Mr. Herron, it is amusing yet pitiful to note the ease with which the most foolish assertions can deceive people.

During the time of his imprisonment, a Christian worker was trying to "undeceive" one of his most ardent followers:

"But how can you believe that Mr. Herron is Christ when the Word distinctly says that His coming will be as the lightning that shineth from the east even unto the west?"

"Why, when Jesus came to earth the first time, He was born in the east, wasn't He?"

"Yes."

"And when Mr. Herron was born, that was in the west, was it not—Detroit is surely in the Western hemisphere!"

How ridiculous! Yet so easily are some led captive by the silly lies of deceivers.

Then, too, there was Annie Besant's pet boy—the "Star of the East," also the "Bab" of Persia—whom so many worshiped as the Christ. While engaged in Christian work in New York City, my mother chanced to room in a house, the landlady of which was absorbed from morning till night in lauding the name of this "Bab," declaring him to be the Christ returned to earth again. Meetings were held to worship him who dwelt across the sea, and, incidentally, to raise money to swell his coffers.

Charles Taze Russell promulgated the doctrine of an invisible return of the Lord in 1874, while many declared the coming of Mary Baker Eddy, with her book *Science and Health with Key to the Scriptures*, to be the coming of the Lord, and their "revelator."

During a winter tent campaign in Florida some years ago, I was preaching joyfully about the second coming of the Lord. So happy and exalted became my heart while declaring the transporting joy of this theme that I cried aloud, "Oh, I will know Him when I see Him, and will follow Him forevermore." During the altar call, while men and women were weeping their way to the front, I made my way down the aisle to personally invite men and women to make this Savior theirs. As I passed a certain seat about halfway down the aisle, a man reached out a detaining hand and laid it upon my arm. Thinking some poor soul needed advice or encouragement, I turned to him.

"Sister?" he said.

"Yes, sir?"

"Did I understand you to say that you believe that Jesus is coming soon and that you are longing to see Him?"

"Oh, yes, sir," I said. "I am sure that He is coming, and I do long to see His face!"

"Did I understand you to say that you would know Him when you saw Him, and would follow Him wherever He should lead?" he persisted.

"Yes, indeed! I am sure that I would know Him amongst 10 million and will walk by His side forever."

"Then I have some good news for you, Sister."

"Is that so?"

"Yes, I have good news for you. I am Jesus Christ. Will you follow me?"

"No, indeed, sir!" I gasped. "I will not follow you. You are not my Jesus, with the pierced hands and side and feet. He will descend in the clouds of heaven with a shout, the voice of an archangel, and the trump of God. And if I am faithful, I will rise to meet Him in midair, so to be ever with the Lord. No, sir, I will not follow you!"

Oh, thank God, none of these are the coming to the Christ but mere fulfillment of the signs that must precede His blessed appearance.

False Prophets

"And many false prophets shall rise, and shall deceive many" (Matthew 24:11). This is the generation in which false prophets and false religions spring up and become firmly rooted overnight.

What church is making the conquests that so-called Christian Science is today? Diabolically hatched in the heart of Satan, denying the deity of Christ and the necessity of cleansing through His precious blood, wrapping its deception in robes of "correct thinking" and "divine love," it comes as an angel of light and plunges ahead in great sweeping strides. Money and people in ever increasing numbers fall into its deceptive lines and follow after. One after another the temples of this false religion rise. Most of them look like great mausoleums, and that is what they are—white sepulchers filled with dead men's bones. Unless they who follow this delusion of the devil renounce its teachings and accept Jesus Christ as the only begotten Son of God, without the shedding of whose precious blood there is no remission of sins (see Hebrews 9:22), they will certainly be lost forever, for only the blood can save.

Spiritualism, the mother of Christian Science, is even less careful to cover its satanic origin and rule. Here, few pretenses to godliness, Christianity, Bible study, or prayer are made. Yet, with their false representations and assertions of being able to call back the departed dead, thousands have been beguiled into their toils. The spirit in which they bring them is unquestionably of the devil. Nor does all spiritualism consist of such hocus pocus as table tipping, mysterious raps, and Ouija boards. The devil has power to impersonate departed spirits and give advice that, if followed, often leads to unspeakable crimes, suicide, and endless damnation. And yet, that these prophecies of Christ might be fulfilled, no less a personage than Sir Oliver Lodge has become one of its chief exponents.

While on the West Coast, both in San Francisco and Los Angeles, I came in contact with a new religion, whose self-given name is the Perfect Christian Divine Way, or P.C.D.W. These people openly worship the devil, declare he is a good fellow, a great jester, a wonderful friend, and in league with God Himself, to test the integrity and faith of mankind. They claim that once we recognize what a harmless fellow the devil is, and accept him as our friend, we will be all right, and our religion will be a joyous one. These people claim biblical authority for their teaching and dress in a garb that somewhat resembles that of a Catholic priest or nun. But they are gaining a following. So bold are they that they entered our meetings and distributed their literature until ordered to stop.

The things that Christian Science and spiritualism do in certain instances are truly miraculous. Does anyone but God have power to perform miracles? Yes, the devil, who caused the magicians' rods to become serpents (see Exodus 7:11–12), has power also, and this power will be displayed more and more in the last days. *"False prophets shall rise, and shall show signs and wonders, to seduce, if it were possible, even the elect"* (Mark 13:22). In Revelation 13:13–14, we read that Satan's powers will be able to call down fire from heaven and deceive those who dwell on the earth by the means of miracles that, through his human instruments and the antichrist, he is able to perform.

Love Waxes Cold

"Because iniquity shall abound, the love of many shall wax cold" (Matthew 24:12). Today, iniquity abounds on every hand. Politics are corrupted; greed, avarice, and moneygrubbing urge the people on; feasting, drinking, dancing; the giddy world of the cabaret; honking automobiles that roll along the streets in splendor; beautiful ladies in whose arms are clasped poodle dogs and from whose

painted lips the blue smoke of a cigarette is breathed. Iniquity abounds; the cup is full of overflowing.

And because iniquity shall abound, the love of many shall wax cold. *"For that day shall not come, except there come a falling away first"* (2 Thessalonians 2:3). This is the day of which Paul spoke, saying men shall have *"a form of godliness, but denying the power thereof: from such turn away"* (2 Timothy 3:5).

Here again is the prophecy fulfilled; one has but to look upon the cold forms and ceremonies of apostate creeds to see it everywhere. Ministers who deny the miracles of the Bible; taboo, supernatural ministers who declare only a part of the sacred Writ is reliable or inspired; ministers who dispute the deity of Christ; dainty, namby-pamby preachers who protest that it is a sickening shock to the refined delicacy of their people to so much as mention the precious blood of Jesus; and ministers who do not believe in "emotionalism" such as altar calls where men and women weep for their sins and are filled with the joy of salvation. God help us to tell the truth about this thing! So many are afraid to preach it! Oh let us get back to the God who lives and saves and answers prayer by fire.

"The love of many shall wax cold." Theological seminaries of today, in whose hands are placed the tender youth who seek training for divine ministry, have become, in many instances, "theological cemeteries," wherein are buried faith in the inspiration of the Scriptures, the story of creation, and the present-day power of God. Theory takes the place of spirituality, and wisdom is made to come from the head instead of living waters from the heart.

How many denominations do you know which once stood against formality and coldness, contending for the old-time religion, but which now have succumbed to the same thing? Today they have become popular—their reproach is taken away, they walk hand in hand with the world, and the devil needs no longer bother fighting them. There have indeed come in these last days *"scoffers, walking after their own lusts, and saying, Where is the promise of his coming?"* (2 Peter 3:3–4).

But praise God, there is a people, in the midst of the people, whose hearts are fixed on God; they are the children of the bridal chamber; their vessels are filled with oil and their lamps are brightly burning. In the iniquity that abounds in the world around them, they see but another milepost pointing to the coming of the Lord. Instead of causing their love to wax cold, these conditions drive them closer to the Lord. In the world and yet not of it (see Romans 12:2), this peculiar, chosen, blood-washed, Spirit-filled company await with intense yearning the coming of their deliverer, and the glorious day when every knee shall bow and every tongue confess that He is Lord (see Romans 14:11).

Knowledge Shall Be Increased

If the increase of knowledge is an indication of the last days (see Daniel 12:4), we are surely living in that time. How often we hear the expression "Really, I do not know how our forefathers existed without the aid of these marvelous labor-saving devices and modern inventions. Why were they not discovered long ago?"

The reason that they were not discovered sooner is that God had a set time for the increase of knowledge—"in the last days." During the last two generations have come the invention of steam locomotives; electrically driven trains; trolleys; electric lights; the telephone; the telegraph; the wireless; cables beneath the sea; the automobile; the airplane; the great coal- and oil-burning steamers that race the sea; the submarine; the giant cannon; the torpedo; the gasoline motor-driven farming implements; the electric motors that do everything from dry hair, rock babies, churn butter, wash clothes, and sweep floors to light whole cities, draw long trains, and lift hundreds of tons. What marvel can surpass the great modern printing press and the linotype machines? Such knowledge, such superhuman genius spring from the minds of two generations—what does it mean? The last days!

"Many Shall Run To and Fro" *(Daniel 12:4)*

Never in the history of the world has it been so easy or customary to travel to and fro as it is today. Transcontinental trains tear across the country day and night, section after section, running within a few minutes of one another. Such trains are taxed to their utmost, and no matter how many more trains are added, officials declare that travel will increase more than ever. Everywhere one goes, railroad depots, docks, ticket offices, and thousands of people are on the move. Thoroughfares and subways are blocked with automobiles; everybody is intent on running to and fro; and the world's on wheels.

The prophet described the automobiles well when he said, *"The chariots shall rage in the streets, they shall justle one against another in the broad ways…they shall run like the lightnings"* (Nahum 2:4).

Wars and Rumors of Wars

And ye shall hear of wars and rumours of wars: see that ye be not troubled: for all these things must come to pass, but the end is not yet.   (Matthew 24:6)

All through the years, since these words were uttered, there have been wars and rumors of wars. From the conquest and fall of Jerusalem in A.D. 70 to the war of the Saxons, the French Revolution, the American Revolution, the Civil War, the Boer War, and the Boxer Rebellion, one international upheaval has followed another. There have been rumors of war with Japan, rumors of wars with Mexico, and the like. But when you see and hear of these things, says Jesus, *"Be ye not troubled: for such things must needs be; but the end shall not be yet"* (Mark 13:7).

The Cry of Peace and Safety

For when they shall say, Peace and safety; then sudden destruction cometh upon them, as travail upon a woman with child; and they shall not escape. (1 Thessalonians 5:3)

For nation shall rise against nation, and kingdom against kingdom: and there shall be famines, and pestilences, and earthquakes, in divers places. (Matthew 24:7)

For many years, the teaching of the second coming of Christ has been revived and taught by some of our most earnest Christians and Bible students. They who taught this wonderful truth declared that, according to God's unfailing Word, certain things must come to pass before He appears. First, there must be a great world war, they said, and then, the Jews must return to their native land. Jerusalem must once again open its gates to the wanderers; earthquakes, famines, bloodshed, and mighty upheavals also must precede and herald that day of days.

The declaration that there must be another and a greater war than was ever known before was met by derision. They cried, "Well, well, the very idea, another war—why, the thing is unthinkable, preposterous! What does the Bible, an old-fashioned book, written hundreds of years ago, know of the twentieth century? What did this Jesus of Nazareth, whose feet walked by the shores of Galilee know of this present age? Of course He had prophesied the war, but *we*—we of the present day—we financiers and politicians are the people to decide this question."

"Indeed, there could not be another great war," declared others. "We are too civilized now to think of entering a barbaric, bloody contest. The pen, which is mightier than the sword, and international arbitration are destined to settle all difficulties between the civilized nations from this time forth."

"War?" scoffed the business men, "Ho! ho! never again!—we will have nothing but peace and safety from this time forth."

For when they shall say, Peace and safety; then sudden destruction cometh upon them…and they shall not escape.

(1 Thessalonians 5:3).

At the dawn of the twentieth century, learned men in the financial, political, and educational world declared that a "world war" would be impossible. "Only weak or morbid minds could seriously entertain such a thought. Who was this Jesus of Nazareth, whose feet walked by the shores of Galilee over nineteen hundred years ago, that He should predict calamities which should envelop the world today? What did the Bible know about our policies, treaties, and amendments? We today are the people to decide these questions with our superior knowledge, our embassies, and our foreign legations," they said with finality.

And so, the cry *"Peace and safety"* sped its way throughout the world. The subject soon became one of international discussion. Newspapers and great journalists devoted pages to the theme of everlasting, universal peace. The army and navy took it up and decided that the best way to keep peace was to prepare for war, to so strengthen their forces with money, men, ships, and munitions that no other nations would dare speak of war.

"Peace!" said the king upon his throne, and settled himself in comfort.

"Peace!" said the magnate in his office, and went on to amass his millions.

"Peace!" said the farmer at his plow, "things will always be as they are."

"Peace!" said the rosy wife as she kissed the sleeping son upon her breast.

"Peace!" cried the youth, and danced in the gilded hall.

"Let's build a palace unto peace," said the nations at their meeting, "a palace built by us all, where leaders of our governments can come together and settle all disputes amicably with the pen, which is mightier than the sword."

And so they built at The Hague, the great "Peace Palace," the most supreme effort ever witnessed, and costing millions. Each nation vied with the other in making costly gifts and donations for its erection. From England came stained glass windows for the council chamber; from France, Gobelin tapestries; from Japan, silk tapestries; from China, priceless porcelain; from Russia, a vase of jasper; from Turkey, costly rugs; from Italy, exquisite marble; from Greece, a marble throne; from the US, marble statuary; from Germany, massive gates of bronze for the park entrance; and from less influential nations, many smaller gifts.

A marvelous library, consisting of some seventy-five thousand volumes on the subject of international peace, was installed. Every international disturbance, its cause, and the method in which it was adjusted, was codified and indexed for immediate reference in future arbitration.

A body of eminent judges was brought together from various parts of the earth and elected to sit as a permanent jury upon each difficulty between the nations. There was to be no more war, they said, as all issues would now be settled amicably by international arbitration.

The palace was completed; the flags of the nations were triumphantly unfurled to the breeze from its turrets and domes; the bands blared forth the national anthems; marching soldiers drew to attention and saluted; all hats were off as thousands cheered, "Hurrah! Hurrah for peace!"

But what was that you said in your Word, Lord? *"When they shall say, Peace and safety; then sudden destruction cometh upon them."*

War

Then, the blow fell.

Like a bolt of lightning from a clear sky, like a tornado on a summer's day, as a destruction from the Almighty did it come.

Feasting was turned into mourning, songs into lamentation. Sublimely unconscious of the rising scepter of death, the godless, dancing, merry multitude went on unheeding till, in one swift moment, the placid sea of *"peace and safety"* was turned into a tempestuous, seething cauldron of hate, fury, and war.

Thirteen declarations of war were made in one month. Six of eight of the greatest world powers were tearing at one another's throats. And as the German hordes went swarming through ravished Belgium, crying, "On to Paris!" people began to recall the words of the Lord: *"For nation shall rise against nation, kingdom against kingdom"* (Matthew 24:7).

Our own fair USA stood for a time beneath its unfurled stars and stripes, gazing with fascinated horror at the bloody carnage of a world gone mad. Wider and wider swept the vortex of the war tornado until we, too, were plunged into the center of its fray.

And signs in the earth beneath; blood, and fire, and vapour of smoke. (Acts 2:19)

Blood? Ah, yes! No need is there to remind the still torn and throbbing heart of the world, of the blood of mothers' sons that stained the fields of Flanders with a deeper dye than the poppies in the dell.

And fire! Yes, there was the fire of belching cannon, the gruesome fire of funeral pyres, the lurid flame of burning towns and villages, and the fire of burning forests that licked the blackness of the night with crimson tongue. Fire? Why, the men even fought each other with sheets and curtains of liquid fire.

And smoke! There rises still before our eyes in vision hazy, smoke-filled battlefields and smoke of guns that were never silent, the smoke of burning homes and homes that lie like ashes smoldering in the dust. On land, men fought with vapors of smoke and poisonous gases; and on sea, men wrapped their ships in curtains of smoke to hide them from hostile eyes.

> *And there shall be famines, and pestilences, and earthquakes,*
> *in divers places.* (Matthew 24:7)

"But how could this prophecy ever be fulfilled, to any marked degree?" protested the Bible critic in the pre-war days. "Look at our fields of waving grain, our gigantic elevators, our cold storage food supplies, our reserve of this and that…." But like every other prophecy in the Word of God, this too must come to pass. Who is there among us who has not shuddered with horror at the pictures and accounts that our daily papers contained, depicting the famine-stricken sufferers of Armenia and other lands?

"And pestilences"—No! "We will never have another great world epidemic," they said, "for our learned medical doctors have discovered serum and antitoxin to destroy almost every known germ." But think for a moment of the plagues of the last generation! Think of the thousands of beautiful children and grown boys and girls, stricken down with infantile paralysis and of the "influenza plague" that came sweeping around the world, leaping the sea on the wings of the wind and beginning its work without a boat to carry it. From the burning sands of Africa's desert to the icy borders of Alaska, through city and country, through the homes of rich and poor, this pestilent, relentless messenger of death spread its wings. Without respect for person or place, it swept on; they with strong, well bodies succumbed as quickly as the weak. No medical skill has been able to determine where it came from or where it went. And yet it took more lives and devastated more homes than all the war. Caskets could not be made quickly enough;

and in large cities, scores were buried in one long grave, awaiting such time as death should stay his hand and a proper burial be made possible.

It has been well and truthfully said that "prophecy is the mold of history." Today, the multitudinous signs foretold in God's Word are being fulfilled on every hand, and, speeding like swift ships of the air, are heralding the coming of Christ.

Today, awakened hearts are throbbing as never before, pulsating with new life and comfort—the near fulfillment of "that blessed hope." The last prayer in the Bible is being breathed from earnest souls, *"Even so, come, Lord Jesus."* Multitudes are crying with Samuel Rutherford, "O day, dawn! O time, run fast! Oh Bridegroom, post, post fast, that we may meet! O heavens, cleave in two, that that bright face and head may set itself through the clouds!"

For centuries, our fathers have foretold and looked forward to this day wherein we live, the day of prophecy fulfilled, the cup of the Gentiles all but full, and the clarion assembly call to Israel's scattered host.

Should anyone ask, however, "Which of the multitudinous signs that are now being fulfilled do you consider the most marvelous and convincing?" we would answer, without hesitation (and I am sure that other writers and thinkers will agree with us), the sign of:

The Fig Tree Putting Forth Her Leaves

Now learn a parable of the fig tree; when his branch is yet tender, and putteth forth leaves, ye know that summer is nigh: so likewise ye, when ye shall see all these things, know that it is near, even at the doors. (Matthew 24:32–33)

The fig tree, as every Bible student knows, represents the Jewish nation and is the emblem of Israel. Prophecies concerning Christ's coming cluster more thickly about the Jew than any other people. Students of the Word have always realized that before His appearing, many great changes must take place with regard to this people in accordance with the fulfillment of Bible prophecy concerning them in this day and age.

They must increase in number. The gates of Palestine must again swing open to admit their weary, wandering, exiled feet. The "unspeakable Turk" must be unseated from the citadel of his power; and his spell of fear and terror broken. The Promised Land, long since but a desert waste, must spring forth into new fertility and blossom as a rose beneath the latter rain. Great wealth must come to this race. Jerusalem must be restored, the seaports opened to make her the center of commerce, and the temple rebuilt.

Improbability of Prophecy's Fulfillment

For generations, these prophecies have been read and pondered, but how unlikely their fulfillment appeared with the many seemingly insurmountable barriers in the way. How could they be brought to pass and this scattered, despised people ever again become a nation, with the Son of David as their King? And even if Turkey's grip was broken and they should return, how could they eke out a living from those barren, sun-bleached hills?

Skeptics laughed the idea to scorn; infidels held such prophecy up to ridicule—a proof that the Bible was not only infallible but had openly, flagrantly erred. "The Promised Land!" laughed Charles Darwin. "Ho! ho! To think of calling that narrow strip of land, those barren hills by the open sea, 'a Promised Land'!" Evidently, Darwin had not read the Bible enough to know that the Promised Land is one-fifth larger than France, and had he ever had a glimpse of California as it is today, he would have seen what a little irrigation can do for a few barren hills by the open sea.

But how could the captivity of Jacob be turned? Persecuted, beaten, crucified, bruised, driven, kicked as a football by the nations—yea, even crucified! How could they be restored to power and influence and home?

In the light of today's illuminating chain of events, let us see if these questions are not being answered and the problems solved one by one.

The Dispersion and Persecution of the Jews

So evident and worldwide has been the dispersion and persecution of the Jew that little need be said along this line. For centuries, beginning with Isaiah, the first of the major prophets, to Malachi, the last of the minor prophets, holy men who spoke as the oracles of God foretold great calamities and catastrophes that were to engulf Jerusalem and the nation.

Higher and higher piled the towering prophetic wave, threatening to break upon them at any moment unless they repented. Yet, in the face of it all, they rejected the God of Abraham, stoned His prophets, and, as the last great culmination of wickedness, crucified His Son, Jesus Christ.

Then the wave broke! The judgment of an outraged God fell upon the masters of that infamy. How little did the murderers realize the meaning of their own words when they mockingly shouted, "*His blood be on us, and on our children*" (Matthew 27:25).

Awesome indeed was the fate of those instrumental in the crucifixion of Christ. His betrayer, Judas Iscariot, hanged himself. The rope broke, and his falling body was burst asunder so that his bowels gushed out. (See Acts 1:18.) History tells us that Herod, who participated in it, was dethroned by Caesar and left to die in infamy and exile; Annas and his household were mobbed and ruined, and his son dragged through the streets, tied to a whipping post, scourged and slain. Pilate, who, like a weakly coward, sat back and allowed it for fear of losing Jewish control and the favor of the people, was stripped of the very things he sought to hold and banished from his country. Tradition says that he soon went in anguish to a suicide's grave from the insufferable shame and ignominy that relentlessly pursued him.

In A.D. 70, Jerusalem was captured by the Romans, and dark prophecy began to be fulfilled. From then till now, the weaving of Palestine's history upon the loom of life has been shaped in the pattern of a cross upon a skull and wrought in somber and sorrowful colorings. Wrath and retribution gripped its people with a mailed fist of steel, and they were made to drink to the dregs the cup of bitter gall and vinegar, which they had but a little time since placed to the Savior's lips. Multitudes were sold into slavery, many for a more miserable pittance than the thirty pieces of silver paid the traitor Judas for betraying the Son of God into their hands.

Many were crucified and tortured as brutally as the Savior they despised. Their portion has been famine, oppression, dispersion, and bloodshed. They who cried, *"Crucify him"* (Mark 15:14; Luke 23:21; John 19:6, 15) have been hated, driven from their own land, hissed, spurned and ostracized by the nations. Their beloved city has been the storm center of war and conquest, political and religious, all down the ages. Someone has said that they who desire to follow the Jew through his years of dispersion will follow a trail of blood. Truly, his blood has been upon them and their children.

Scattered! Yes, according to prophecy, they were to be scattered "like corn through a fine sieve." Could their dispersion be more adequately described? Go where you may today, you will find the scattered sons of Jacob. So persecuted and ruthlessly slaughtered were they that one hundred years ago, there were estimated to be only some 200,000 Jews in the world.

But through the centuries, hear the voice of Jehovah, who never changes:

> *What have I here, saith the* LORD, *that my people is taken away for nought? they that rule over them make them to howl, saith the* LORD; *and my name continually every day is blasphemed. Therefore my people shall know my name: therefore they shall know in that day that I am he that doth speak: behold, it is I.*   (Isaiah 52:5–6)

Startling Increase in Number

That they have entered upon a new era can be readily realized since statistics rate their number at 15 million. What a startling increase it is!

In the Middle Ages, when the great Jewish traveler Benjamin of Tudela visited Jerusalem, he found there just four Jews. Today, they form the majority of its population. When the Jews gain a foothold in a city, they soon increase and spread till former residents and merchants are pushed back and out, and a Jewish colony is formed and firmly rooted.

Russia, despite her slaughter and cruelty, is said to contain more than 6 million Jews today; Turkey, seventy-five thousand; Austria-Hungary, more than 2 million; France, one hundred thousand; Germany, six hundred and fifteen thousand; and Morocco, three hundred thousand. There are Jewish colonies and synagogues in the cities of China, in the heart of Africa, and in the desert itself. When the Portuguese settled in India some years ago, they found three distinct colonies of Jews there. When England took possession of Aden, she found more Jews than Gentiles.

London has a huge Jewish population. New York City contained 1.5 million Jews at the close of the war. Detroit has fifty thousand; Chicago, two hundred and twenty-five thousand; Philadelphia, two hundred thousand; Cleveland, one hundred thousand. Our own country contains some 3.5 million of these wandering exiles.[1]

Distinct and Unassimilated

Without a doubt, they are the greatest, most absorbingly interesting nation in the world today—existing without a king or queen, a flag, a government, or a land.

They live in our midst, one of the oldest races on earth, and, refusing to intermarry, have kept their blood relatively pure. The religions of the world have not made the slightest impression upon them. One writer declares,

There now exists a nation on the earth which for forty centuries alone of all the peoples of the world, forms one family, and has descended from one father the only one which has kept its nationality in the midst of upheavals, of massacres, and of expulsions, through all the ages; under Nebuchadnezzar, and under Charlemagne and Napoleon, and under empires that have passed away as a shadow, leaving only their names. These empires have perished and their places know them no more; but the Jew remains, standing apart from all other nations, distinct, unique; a thousand times despoiled, and yet rich, constantly slain, and yet ever increasing in numbers; dispersed to the ends of the earth, but more and more united.

Thus, going back to Jerusalem, they will be thrown up on the shores of Palestine, a separate, distinct nation, intact and unassimilated as was Jonah from the belly of the whale. Ordinarily, the

1. Numbers based on population circa 1920.

great fish would have assimilated the body of Jonah, but he was chosen, foreordained, protected, chastened by God, and thrown back whole to do His bidding and fulfill His Word.

So the Jewish nation, though swallowed up in the angry, insatiable maw of the nations subjected to the acid tests of the world with its manifold religions and intermingling of races, has been kept intact as a nation and will be thrown up whole on the shores of Palestine, a living testimony to the truth of God's immutable Word.

4

THE JEWISH QUESTION
AND HOW TO SOLVE IT

The world has always had a Jewish question, and always will, till this persecuted, scattered nation finds a resting place in a land of its own, and gathers around the throne of David.

The high notes of pathos, truth, and logic were struck most convincingly by the Jewish writer D. de Solo Pool, when he wrote in 1916:

> What does the world mean when it talks about the Jewish problem?
>
> The people of Russia talk of a Jewish problem in Russia. The Poles talk of a Jewish problem in Poland. Englishmen talk of a Jewish problem in England, and the people of the United States are beginning to talk of a Jewish problem in the United States.
>
> Why should we Jews everywhere be a problem to the rest of the world? The Russian is not a problem in Russia,

the Pole is not a problem in Poland, nor the Englishman in England, nor the American in the United States. No people is a problem in its own land. It is only the people of foreign race in a land who are a problem to that land. For example, the Japanese and the Chinese who are settled in the Western States of the United States constituted no problem while in their own lands. But since they have come in large numbers to California and other Western States, they have become a serious problem to the United States.

...

The situation is rendered the more painful for us because of the fact that we have no homeland of our own in which we can settle without being a problem to someone else. In whatever remote corner of the world we choose to settle in appreciable numbers, we are always strange to the people of the land so long as we remain Jews, and we are therefore everywhere generating local outbreaks of the Jewish problem. In this way, as we have been scattered North, South, East and West, we have carried the Jewish problem with us all over the world. Whither can we go to escape persecution? Whither can we flee to be free of anti-Semitism? Wherever we go, prejudice and anti-Semitism follow us. We are a people without a home, a race of wandering Jews looking everywhere in vain for rest. If the Japanese is not welcomed in California, he may go back to Japan. If the Hindu is not permitted to enter Canada, he may return to India, where he is at home. Other peoples of the world can escape becoming a problem to their neighbors by the simple expedient of staying at home in their own lands. We only are compelled to be a problem to our neighbors everywhere, because we have no home land to which we may retire or in which we may remain.

Dr. Theodor Herzl and other Jewish thinkers who founded the modern Zionist movement, therefore said to the nations of the world: The real solution of your Jewish problem lies in giving back to us Jews our homeland. Not all the Jews would return to this land, and you would not rid yourselves of all your Jews. But you would relieve yourselves of your acute Jewish problem by making it possible for many Jews to emigrate to their homeland in order to escape ill will....We wish to avoid being driven round the world in a vicious circle, like schnorrers who are sent on from village to village and from town to town because no one wishes them to stay and no one gives them a welcome. If therefore, you nations of the world really wish to know how to solve this Jewish problem, which seems to you to be so difficult and which troubles you so sorely, we can tell you how this can be done very simply: give to us or sell to us or allow us to gain control of our own homeland so that we need not crowd into your lands. You will then be the happier and we shall be the happier....There is only one land that we call ours, and that is the land of our hope, the land of our ancestors, the land made sacred by our past and by our Bible, by all our traditions, by our prayers and our tears, the Promised Land, the land of Palestine. If we can be given the opportunity to make that land our own, we shall solve for you the Jewish problem of which you complain.

Zionist Movement

Since the destruction of the temple nearly two thousand years ago, the longing for Palestine has been ever present with the Jews. They have never ceased to recall their past, mourn for its loss, and daily pray for a future that should bury the very memory of that calamity in the glories of a restored national life. It was the hope of a return to the land of his fathers that buoyed up the Jew amidst persecution, and for the realization of which the devout ever prayed. Until a generation ago, this was merely a hope—a wish piously prayed over but not worked for. But the rebirth of the Jewish nation is no longer a dream. It is in process of fulfillment in a most practical way, and the story is a wonderful one. Today we gaze upon the fascinating spectacle of a nation buried for two thousand years in dispersion and martyrdom, shaking off the graveclothes and rising from the dead.

From the midst of this death, Israel, two thousand years dead, has arisen no longer a race among the races but once more a nation among nations.

To Chaim Weizmann, more than to any other one man, fell the task of conducting the negotiations that brought the British Empire to its outright Zionist public pledge.

There has gradually come about a change in the outlook of the Jew—a change that can be more easily felt by those who are in touch with Jewish affairs than by those who measure it by facts and figures. This change is illustrated most concretely by the growth of the Zionist organization itself, with its two hundred thousand adherents in all parts of the world, its biennial representative congresses, its network of financial institutions, its press in many languages, and its incessant and extensive propaganda by the written and spoken word.

The possibilities of a Jewish resettlement of Palestine, the land which forms the connecting link of three continents and three religions, are incalculable, whether looked at from the political, economic, or religious point of view.

In our own generation, we have lived to see the birth and rise of the Zionist Movement—its purpose being to restore Israel to

Palestine. Jew and Gentile alike are digging deeply in their pockets to abet the cause that but a few years ago was pronounced unlikely and even impossible. The smoldering hope cherished in the heart of Israel Zangwill, Jewish writer and political activist, and of countless thousands has today burst forth into leaping, exultant flames of joy. Hopes long deferred are being realized at last. A quota of 10 million dollars is even now being raised for the express purpose of rebuilding Jerusalem and restoring a national Jewish home in Palestine. Over two billion dollars have been raised for the relief of suffering and famine-stricken Jews in Armenia and other lands—30 million from Greater New York alone.

The Fig Leaves of Education

The fig leaves of education are budding forth. One Jewish writer, in discussing the Jews' progress in the educational and business world, says of his brethren, "They have wormed their way into appointments and into the free professions by dint of pliancy, mock humility, mental acuteness, and clandestine protection. If struck or spat upon by 'Aryan' students, they rarely ventured to return the blow or the insult." Through all the sweat and all the grime of their daily scrambles on the slopes of their slippery ghetto pit, they have won out and up to ideas and ideals. Beyond all proportion, the Jews of today are the financiers, politicians, scientists, university professors, ambassadors, and congressmen.

Six of our most prominent members of Congress are Jews—representatives from New York, Chicago, Indiana, San Francisco, and so forth. Among the many prominent leading men of today and yesterday might be mentioned the following members of Congress—Levy, Simon, Strauss, Wolf, and Yulee. In passing, mention might also be made of the following well-known Jews in Who's Who Today: Abram Elkus of New York, ambassador to Turkey in 1916–17, who is now judge of the court of appeals in the State of New York; Louis Marshall of New York, chairman of American Jewish Relief, trustee of Syracuse University since 1910, to which he presented a Law Library, also president of New York State College of Forestry; Cyrus Adler and J. Henry Schiff, founders and professors of theological seminaries and colleges; Louis D. Brandeis, Washington, DC, justice of the Supreme Court of the United States, counsel for the government in the Riggs National Bank case, 1915, scientific manager of labor problems and trusts; Simon Wolf, minister to Egypt under the Cleveland administration; Julius Rosenwald of Chicago, civic philanthropist and supporter of educational enterprises, who contributed $700,000 to the University of Chicago alone; Baron Sonnino, minister of foreign affairs in Italy.

We will not take space to enumerate others famous in history, chemistry, art, and music, though such names as Rubinstein, Mendelssohn, Isaac D'Israeli, Jascha Heifetz, Mischa Elman, and Efram Zimbalist will ever be recorded on the annals of great geniuses.

England has a Jewish chief justice and governor general.

It is said that eight chairs of the Chicago University are filled by Jewish professors and that half the faculty of Columbia University are of this race.

There are seventy-six national Jewish organizations in the United States.

Some of the greatest modern scientific discoveries of the day have been made by Jews. We are told that when England first entered the recent war, she had not the formulas for the much-needed high explosives. A prominent Jewish scientist provided her with them, and when asked to name the price for so valuable a gift, requested only that should Great Britain and the Allied armies capture Palestine, they would restore it to the Jews.

The Fig Leaf of Finance

The fig leaf of finance is being put forth upon this tree today. Though millions of them are still suffering and poor in Europe, the Jews are rapidly becoming the people of greatest wealth and influence in the world.

Some realization of their financial status and strength was brought forcibly to mind during the trying of the Dreyfus case in Paris some years ago. A second trial was demanded, but France refused it. So thoroughly did the Jews control the wealth of Europe that stocks and bonds suddenly began to drop, and French financiers to tremble lest the financial backbone of the country should be broken across the knees of Jewish finances. As a last resort, the trial was given, and stocks and bonds came back to normal.

If you are ever in lower Broadway or Wall Street on a Jewish holiday, you will be startled into a realization of the tremendous grasp they have upon the finances of our country—business, markets, and the stock exchange are practically at a standstill.

It is a common saying that the Jews own the USA. Even before the war, there were said to be in New York City fifty-three banking houses owned and controlled by the Jews and 115 millionaire Jews. Rothschild alone is estimated to be worth 482 million.

Three Major Fig Leaves Appear in Recent World War

Among the manifold leaves appearing so rapidly upon the fig tree, there are none perhaps that can be considered of more major importance than:

1. The routing of the unspeakable Turk
2. The capture of Jerusalem by Great Britain

3. The unfurling of the Union Jack, which now floats triumphantly over Jerusalem

The recent world war surely marked the beginning of the end of the times of the Gentiles. Had it accomplished nothing else than the elementary simmering down of the old Roman nations to the ten toes of Daniel's image and the opening of Palestine's gates to the Jew, the world conflict would have been a most marvelous fulfillment of prophecy.

The Capture of Jerusalem

Through the long-drawn, tortuous months, which dragged leaden footed into years—years of anguish and death—the battle went hard and long. To and fro, back and forth, surged the weary lines, now gaining, now losing, grimly, fiercely hanging on.

Meanwhile, the fighting spread and encompassed the Holy Land. The dislodgment of Turks from Europe became one of the great subjects of the day, entailing as it did Jerusalem and the fate of Israel. It was then that Arthur James Balfour, British foreign secretary, and other men of influence made the promise that "if the Allies conquer, they will stand pledged to the erection of a Jewish state in Palestine."

"His Majesty's government view with favour the establishment in Palestine of a national home for the Jewish people, and will use their best endeavours to facilitate the achievement of this object." Thus wrote Arthur Balfour of England to the Jews on November 2, 1917. And on February 12, 1918, France said, "So be it." Italy followed on May 9, 1918, and other Allied governments and men of light leading the world over said, "Amen"; and the dream of the Jewish people thus became one of the war aims of the Allied Powers. The doubters smiled and said of the British declaration, "A scrap of paper! Will the act follow the word?"

But this was the turning point of the war. Within one month, General Allenby and his troops encamped without the city walls, waiting for the break of day and the formal capture of Jerusalem.

The morning broke. The battalions fell into line. Airships buzzed and roared as they circled overhead. "Forward march!" rang the command.

Then, as with fixed bayonets and uncovered heads, the Allied soldiers entered the gates and marched through the streets, and the Turks fell back unresisting, step-by-step. Not a single shot was fired or opposition offered.

> *For thus hath the* LORD *spoken unto me, Like as the lion and the young lion roaring on his prey, when a multitude of shepherds is called forth against him, he will not be afraid of their voice, nor abase himself for the noise of them: so shall the* LORD *of hosts come down to fight for mount Zion, and for the hill thereof.*   (Isaiah 31:4)

How wonderfully God had staged the whole setting for the wondrous drama enacted that day. Was not even the presence and the battle formation of the airplanes that encircled Jerusalem and filled the skies like a cloud of huge and angry birds foretold in the Word of God? "*As birds flying, so will the* LORD *of hosts defend Jerusalem; defending also he will deliver it; and passing over he will preserve it*" (Isaiah 31:5).

It was on December 10, 1917, that the Allied army led by the British captured Jerusalem and later conquered the southern half of Palestine for the Jewish people. British Jews and those of other Allied lands were enabled to join the Jewish legion and take part in the liberation of their land for their people. Even now, in Palestine, a Jewish Administrative Commission, acting under the authority of the British Government and with the assistance of the British military staff, is organizing the foundations of the Jewish homeland.

Thus, with one breath from God, the whole thing was accomplished. With one turn of His hand did He direct the wheels of His chariot, prophecy and history running neck and neck, swift, sure-footed, obedient steeds beneath the guidance of His eye.

The Bible is indeed the most up-to-date book in the world. Its news is accurate, reliable, and ahead of time.

Man thought he had made a new and remarkable discovery when he found that the world was round, but God's Word had known it all the time, plainly declaring that at Christ's second coming, two shall be sleeping in one bed (on the side of the earth where it will be night), while on the other (where it will be broad daylight), two women shall be grinding at the mill. (See Luke 17:34–35).

Again in the case of Sargus and its king, Bible critics derided the term and description, boldly affirming that there had never been such a place or king. They were rather chagrined, however, when during recent excavations, a portion of the old city was unearthed and tablets of stone bearing record of the king himself were found. The Bible is verily the most up-to-date book in the world, and centuries ahead of the latest editions of the most modern scientists and learned men.

And so it is in the history of the Jew, if you would be abreast of the times, well informed, able to speak wisely, with assurance and certainty of their future—read the Bible, and thus get the advanced news, the most authentic information.

The Return of the Jews to Jerusalem

Today the gates stand open wide—a welcoming hand is extended. All through the centuries, the longing of the Jews to return to their own land has lived on and on from generation to generation. A very significant item appeared in a recent publication: "The next time you are in London," says the writer, "go along by Hyde Park, look at the second house by the gate. Notice the marble pillars and the cornice above; one of them is unfinished. This is the home of Lord Rothschild, perhaps the richest man in the world. He is an orthodox Jew, and every orthodox Jew, when building his house, leaves a portion unfinished, bearing testimony to the fact that he is but a pilgrim and knows that he is not in a permanent abiding place."

Will the Jews return, you ask? Yes, indeed, for even today the Word of the Lord is being fulfilled before your eyes. Ships are being chartered to speed them on their way. Russia and new Germany are taking active steps to expedite their departure.

> *Therefore fear thou not, O my servant Jacob, saith the* Lord; *neither be dismayed, O Israel: for, lo, I will save thee from afar, and thy seed from the land of their captivity; and Jacob shall return, and shall be in rest, and be quiet, and none shall make him afraid. For I am with thee, saith the* Lord, *to save thee: though I make a full end of all nations whither I have scattered thee, yet I will not make a full end of thee: but I will correct thee in measure, and will not leave thee altogether unpunished.* (Jeremiah 30:10–11)

> *Sing with gladness for Jacob, and shout among the chief of the nations: publish ye, praise ye, and say, O* Lord, *save thy people, the remnant of Israel. Behold, I will bring them from the north country, and gather them from the coasts of the earth, and with them the blind and the lame…a great company shall return thither. They shall come with weeping, and with supplications will I lead them…for I am a father to Israel, and Ephraim is my firstborn. Hear the word of the* Lord, *O ye nations, and declare it in isles afar off, and say, He that scattered Israel will gather him, and keep him, as a shepherd doth his flock.* (Jeremiah 31:7–10)

Palestine Idea Sweeps Breadth of Land as Restoration Work Engages All Jewry

The following clippings from the press of recent issues give some idea of the tremendous movements of the Jews toward Jerusalem and the fulfillment of Bible prophecy.

Half a Million Siberian Jews Eager to Migrate to Palestine

From *The New Palestine*:

Over 90 percent of the entire Jewish population of China, Japan, Siberia and Russian Manchuria are anxiously awaiting an opportunity to migrate to Palestine, according to Samuel Mason, Jewish Relief Commissioner to Siberia, whose report on this remarkable situation was made public by the Zionist Organization of America.

"The same tense yearning is found among the Jewish communities of Siberia proper and the Ural," says Mr. Mason.

"In Japan there is no Zionist organization of any description, yet there are hundreds of Jews there, 95 per cent of the Jewish population impatiently awaiting the time when they may have their passports visaed, so that they can embark in Mediterranean steamships for Palestine. This mass desire to emigrate to Palestine which I found everywhere in the East is not due to propaganda, but is an expression of deeply ingrained Jewish sentiment."

The thousands of Jews in the Far East waiting for the opening of Palestine through the establishment of the League of Nations or the signing of the treaty with Turkey are roughly grouped into five classes by

Mr. Mason—investors, traders, farmers, laborers, and idealists.

"The traders contain a large proportion of men with extensive export and import business experience, which they propose to utilize on a large scale in Palestine. Several corporations with capitalizations of millions of rubles for the purpose of exporting and importing materials to Asia Minor via Palestine have already been formed at Harbin and Irkutsk. A shipping company has been established at Harbin.

"The farmers want to convert their Russian currency into agricultural implements as soon as they know they can proceed, and that there is available land for them."

Estimates Million Jews Preparing to Leave Russian for Palestine

Dr. Alexander Salkind, former president of the Jewish Community of Petrograd, at present member of the Jewish National Council of the Ukraine, and now visiting America, brings with him fresh news of Jewish conditions in Russia.

Those who have not lately been among the Jews of the Ukraine and White Russia can hardly form an idea of the feelings which dominate them. Rich and poor, old and young, women and children—all are carried away by the idea of going to Palestine. The rich want to invest their capital there; the poor hope to be able to find a market for their labor; and the intellectuals hope to be able to apply their knowledge to the building up of the new Palestine. Many have liquidated their property, settled their accounts, and made themselves ready to go. The offices of the Palestine

Commission established by the Zionist Bureau in Kieff are always thronged with hundreds of Jews inquiring as to the possibility of going to Palestine. Deputations which came to Kieff from various communes in the Ukraine while making the usual inquiries declared that other communities had decided to emigrate to Palestine en masse with all their institutions—Cantors, Rabbis, Dayanim, Charities, etc., and that they only wanted to know when the first steamer would leave. Similar deputations are being sent to other big towns, more especially to Odessa, by the smaller places in the Ukraine.

There is no risk of exaggeration in assuming that several thousands, perhaps a million people, are preparing to leave Russia at the first opportunity; and in order to prevent a catastrophe, effective measures must be taken to check the stream of immediate emigration by propaganda and publications of a general character to organize future emigration on a large scale by creating suitable institutions for carrying on the work and to prepare Palestine for receiving the largest possible number of settlers.

Palestine Their One Hope

The following is clipped from an article by Morris Rothenberg in *The Maccabean:*

That the Jews in Eastern Europe realize their intolerable situation is clear from the fact that the largest majority of them are beginning to look toward Palestine as their only hope for the future. From indisputable sources it appears that hundreds of thousands of Jews in Poland, Ukraine, Galicia, and Austria are ready at a moment's notice to migrate to Palestine. In the large centers of Warsaw,

Cracow, Odessa, and Constantinople, there are tens of thousands of Jews who have poured in with their families from the interior of these countries, having sold all their belongings on their way to Palestine. And the very serious problem has arisen to hold back these great numbers until Palestine is ready to receive them. But it is like holding back the waves. The irresistible tide of events is sweeping them from their old moorings toward a new haven of rest, for their present lot is no longer endurable.

A homeland for the Jewish people is therefore not only a spiritual need but an immediate physical necessity. Some have looked with discouragement upon the fact that Palestine is a denuded and a devastated land. But that is precisely the most favorable circumstance for the building of a truly Jewish country. As if by the hand of Providence, this land of our ancestors has not wedded itself to any of the numberless races and tribes that have been in Palestine during the past twenty centuries. They have all come and passed through the land and left it undeveloped. The soil would not respond to alien hands. Not until the first Jewish pioneers, thirty-five years ago, came into Palestine and laid their fingers on the soil did it become fertile; for it felt again the tender touch of those who loved it and cherished it throughout the ages even while in distant lands. Because Palestine is uncultivated will it be possible for the Jews to build in such a manner as will lay the foundations for a truly Jewish life? It will not be necessary to unmake or to dislodge old institutions that have their root in the ground, nor to compel the withdrawal of those who have planted their traditions in the soil. It will be possible to fashion such a life as the Jews desire, to create those forms which are of the essence of the Jewish soul.

To Preserve Jerusalem as a Shrine for all the World

Experts of the Zionist Commission are already engaged in planning a modern scientific city outside the walls, while preserving and beautifying the sites sacred to civilization within the ancient gates. Expert and experienced city builders under the direction of Patrick Geddes have been sent from England to supervise the work, and unlimited means are being placed at their disposal by the wealthiest Jews in the world. Excavations are already being made, reaching down to the old, original floor of Solomon's temple, which is to be rebuilt.

From the *Washington Times*:

A brilliant plan to make ancient Jerusalem the most attractive and prosperous city in the world is already in process of execution. Under this scheme, the incomparable features of the ancient city will be preserved absolutely intact, while around it will be built a thoroughly modern city of the American type, with skyscrapers, trolley cars, modern hotels, drainage, water supply, factories, theatres, and everything that could be desired.

Thus the resident or visitor will be able to enjoy the opportunity of examining when he pleases the world's most sacred and picturesque city, while living under conditions of modern comfort.

The location of Jerusalem was chosen in incalculably early times on account of its defensive position at the summit of a range of high hills. It has never had any drainage system or a satisfactory water supply, and it would be nearly impossible to give these desirable adjuncts. In the surrounding territory, where the modern city will be built, it will be quite easy to furnish these things.

The International Zionist Commission, of which some leading Hebrews of England, France, and America are members, have general control of the work of rebuilding Jerusalem. They are very broad-minded in their views, for they have chosen Prof. Patrick Geddes of St. Andrews University, Scotland, to be chief director of the work on the spot.

Professor Geddes and Dr. Weizmann, head of the British Zionist Commission, have already left for Palestine and are working out plans for rebuilding not only Jerusalem but also Jaffa, Haifa, and other towns. Professor Geddes is an expert in town planning, sociology, and civics. He has already carried out successful town planning in India.

Professor Geddes will establish a university in rebuilt Jerusalem on the lines of a Scottish university.

The Zionist Commission intends to send Zionist colonies to Palestine, some of which will be settled in the rebuilt cities and others in the rural districts.

It need hardly be said that the rebuilding of Jerusalem is a work of unparalleled interest to the whole civilised world—for this city witnessed the supreme act of the Christian religion and contained the sacred temple of the Hebrews, after whose destruction they were condemned to become wanderers upon the earth.

The walls of the city remain much as they were in Hebrew times, although they have been several times moved in some localities. And the Golden Gate still stands, through which a legend says that the Savior will return to rule the city. The enormous foundations of the temple walls and their ramparts are likewise intact.

Without the walls, the old features are still less changed. There stands the Mount of Olives practically as it was in the days of the Savior, and on it is still preserved the garden of Gethsemane, scene of the most fateful mental agony in the world's history, and legend even identifies the sacred footprints.

The Mount of Olives, treated as a park, will form the most beautiful feature of the modern city to be built around the ancient one.

Many experts admit that Jerusalem can be built into a prosperous capital and commercial center. It is a convenient point for the handling of commerce from large parts of Asia Minor. Palestine itself promises to be very productive under suitable cultivation, and in parts of the country there are deposits of oil, which is the most desirable natural product in the world today.

Schools and Colleges in the Holy Land

A complete system of Hebrew education has been developed from kindergarten to high school. The diploma of this high school (the Hebrew Gymnasium of Jaffa) is accepted for admission to Columbia and other American as well as European universities. In addition, there is a technical school at Haifa, the Bezalel School of Arts and Craft at Jerusalem and a music school at Jaffa. Every colony has its elementary schools, hospital, library, and assembly hall. Plans are completed for the opening of a Hebrew University at Jerusalem to be established as soon as practicable on the Mount of Olives.

Hebrew a Dead Language for 2,000 Years Now Resurrected

Perhaps the most extraordinary achievement of Jewish nationalism is the revival of the Hebrew language....The

Hebrew tongue, called a dead language for nearly 2,000 years, has, in the Jewish colonies and in Jerusalem, become again the living mother tongue. The effect of this common language in unifying the Jews is, of course, great; for the Jews of Palestine came literally from all the lands of the earth, each speaking, excepting those who used Yiddish, the language of the country from which he came, and remaining in the main almost a stranger to the other Jews.

By common consent, Hebrew became the language of the colonies. It was the one language that Jews from all parts of the world revered and of which they knew at least a few words in common. From this, by a perfectly natural process, it has become the language of daily life. Men use Hebrew in their commerce and children in their play.

The Fertility of the Land

But what of the barren land? Can it ever be made to yield, and the field to bring forth her fruitage again? Verily, indeed, for here again is prophecy being fulfilled:

Be not afraid, ye beasts of the field: for the pastures of the wilderness do spring, for the tree beareth her fruit, the fig tree and the vine do yield their strength. Be glad then, ye children of Zion, and rejoice in the LORD your God: for he hath given you the former rain moderately, and he will cause to come down for you the rain, the former rain, and the latter rain in the first month. And the floors shall be full of wheat, and the vats shall overflow with wine and oil.   (Joel 2:22–24)

The desert shall rejoice, and blossom as the rose....And the parched ground shall become a pool, and the thirsty land springs of water.   (Isaiah 35:1, 7)

Today, water piped a great distance is supplying the city of Jerusalem, and aqueducts long unused have been discovered. Besides this, the rainfall is being gradually increased month by month. At times, the increase will be an inch, an inch and three-quarters, two inches, and so forth, but ever steadily increasing.

There is enough fall to the river Jordan to permit the building of five great dams the size of those now used for the irrigation of California. The river Titus, flowing high along the ridge, and the snow of the northern hills can easily be brought down by a simple irrigating process, and the desert land, ever fertile and rich in soil, be caused to literally blossom as a rose.

The first pioneers forty years ago struggled with barren and swampy soil, fought malaria, death, disease, and the wild Bedouin. So marvelously did the Palestinian soil respond to the touch of loving hands that even before the war, forty-eight flourishing Jewish colonies had been established, producing wines, olive oil, bamboo, rubber, cotton, tea, oranges, almonds, and all kinds of cereals. The Jewish Colonial Trust, through the Anglo-Palestine Company of Jaffa, with its branches in Jerusalem, Haifa, Bairuth, Hebron, Safed, and Tiberias, with its capital of over 1.25 million dollars and deposits of over 2 million, has been effectively financing the agricultural and industrial needs. Jewish agriculture in Palestine is experimental, adventurous, and scientific.

Aaron Aaronsohn is the head of the "Jewish Agricultural Experiment Station" at Athlit. It has created five new species of wheat and barley especially adapted to the climate of Palestine. It has developed a grape which will ripen three weeks earlier than the grapes of Smyrna and of Cyprus.

Among the products of the country were wines of such excellence that they have been awarded at French expositions, and this in competition with the French products. The value of the vineyards in 1914 amounted to 2,800,000 francs. The wine cellars of the colony Rishon LeZion, built through the munificence of Baron Edmond de Rothschild, are among the largest in the world. The value of its olive orchards in 1914 amounted to 1,380,000 francs. The oranges of Palestine found a ready market in Marseilles, Liverpool, and London, and in the same year, the orange orchards were valued at 10,780,000 francs. The value of the almond groves in the same period amounted to 5,550,000 francs.

The whole flood tide of prophecies as to this very fertility bears us to one sure and certain end, and to one inevitable conclusion: the fig tree is in this day and generation putting forth her leaves; the summer is nigh; the coming King is even at the door. With uplifted, wistful, yearning hearts, we are crying, "Even so, come, Lord Jesus."

Beyond a doubt, we are living in the last days. Man has almost crossed the great continent of time lying between Christ's ascension and His second coming. We press today to the further verge of the present dispensation; and scanning the sea of space that stretches between us and the eternal shores of the New Jerusalem, we look for the glorious appearing of our Lord and Savior Jesus Christ.

In the hands of the faithful, waiting church and of the awakened Bible student, is the Word of God. The eyes of those who look for the Lord are upon it. It is an hour glass, through which the sands of prophecy concerning His coming have nearly all passed. A great bulk, they lie in the bottom of the glass. Those yet to be fulfilled are very few and are slipping with an infinitely steady, swift precision, without a moment's hesitancy, like a silver stream through the narrow space of present fulfillment, adding their weight to those which have gone before them.

There is a great stirring among the children in the bride chamber. The months of preparation in oil and myrrh and frankincense are almost over. The bride is soon to be summoned to go in unto the King. White robes, inwrought with fine needlework of gold of Ophir, are being put upon her. There is a great filling of lamps with Holy Spirit oil. The flame of their lighted truth flashes the message to the dormant worldlings round about. Earthly ties are being severed, weights and shorelines laid aside; longing eyes are lifted skyward, knowing well that soon from the sea of heaven's infinite vastness, they will hear the bursting music of myriad angel harps, that soon will come sailing to earth the glorious, majestic, golden ship of state—bearing the kingly Bridegroom with ten thousand angel hosts to take His loved one home.

But in spite of the well-run sands of the hour glass, in spite of the flashing lamps and warning cries, millions of sleepers lie wrapped in the drunken torpor of revelry and sordid things of the earth. The piercing cry of the watchman means nothing to them. They grin stupidly, uncomprehendingly, when in letters of fire "JESUS IS COMING SOON—GET READY!" is flashed across the sky. They have lived so long in the world of jests and unreality that this, too, seems but mockery—vague before the dullness of their comprehension.

The great King of heaven, whose sumptuous wedding supper is being spread, has noted the numbers of awakened and ready guests, all down the ages. He speaks today from heaven, saying, "Go out into the hedges and highways and compel still others to come in, that my house may be full." What is to be done must be done quickly, for soon, O soon, will the prophecy be fulfilled wherein our Lord shall reign upon the throne of David. The cup of the Gentiles full; the catching up of the bride to meet the Lord in the air; times, times, and half a time of tribulation such as the world has never known; the deception of the Jews by the antichrist (for they will be grossly deceived by the antichrist, through the rejection of their true King, Jesus Christ, and their present great expectancy of the Messiah)—then will the Lord return with

His saints to reign a thousand years, King of Kings and Lord of Lords.

> *Awake, awake; put on thy strength, O Zion; put on thy beautiful garments, O Jerusalem, the holy city: for henceforth there shall no more come into thee the uncircumcised and the unclean.* (Isaiah 52:1)

But alas! never as a nation will they believe or be loosed from their bands of unbelief and its dark consequences, until He shall visibly, literally return in the clouds of heaven, the mighty King of heaven and earth—the King of the Jews.

What will be the feeling in the heart of the Jews when after all their centuries of doubt, disobedience, rejection, and punishment, they shall see the Christ whom they crucified returning in glory that outshines the sun in its dazzling noonday splendor!

> *Then shall appear the sign of the Son of man in heaven: and then shall all the tribes of the earth mourn, and they shall see the Son of man coming in the clouds of heaven with power and great glory.* (Matthew 24:30)

> *Behold, he cometh with clouds; and every eye shall see him, and they also which pierced him: and all kindreds of the earth shall wail because of him. Even so, Amen.* (Revelation 1:7)

> *He shall be great, and shall be called the Son of the Highest: and the Lord God shall give unto him the throne of his father David: and he shall reign over the house of Jacob for ever; and of his kingdom there shall be no end.* (Luke 1:32–33)

> *For unto us a child is born, unto us a son is given: and the government shall be upon his shoulder: and his name shall be called Wonderful, Counsellor, The mighty God, The*

everlasting Father, The Prince of Peace. Of the increase of his government and peace there shall be no end, upon the throne of David, and upon his kingdom, to order it, and to establish it with judgment and with justice from henceforth even for ever. The zeal of the LORD *of hosts will perform this.*

(Isaiah 9:6–7)

[Then shall He say,] *"Break forth into joy, sing together, ye waste places of Jerusalem: for the* LORD *hath comforted his people, he hath redeemed Jerusalem. The* LORD *hath made bare his holy arm in the eyes of all nations; and all the ends of the earth shall see the salvation of our God.*

(Isaiah 52:9–10)

Now learn a parable of the fig tree; when his branch is yet tender, and putteth forth leaves, ye know that summer is nigh: so likewise ye, when ye shall see all these things, know that it is near, even at the doors.   (Matthew 24:32–33)

5

FOR WHOM
IS HE COMING?

*What are these which are arrayed in white robes? and whence
came they? And I said unto him, Sir, thou knowest. And he
said to me, These are they which came out of great tribulation, and have washed their robes, and made them white in
the blood of the Lamb. Therefore are they before the throne
of God, and serve him day and night in his temple: and he
that sitteth on the throne shall dwell among them. They shall
hunger no more, neither thirst any more; neither shall the sun
light on them, nor any heat. For the Lamb which is in the
midst of the throne shall feed them, and shall lead them unto
living fountains of waters: and God shall wipe away all tears
from their eyes.* (Revelation 7:13–17)

What a glorious vision John must have beheld—thousands and
thousands of redeemed saints, sweeping triumphantly over the last
stretch of the journey, clad in white and glistering garments, with

palms of victory, and crowns of joy upon their heads, upturned faces, suffused by the light that streams upon them through wide-flung gates.

And just beyond, through gates of solid pearl, lies the Celestial City. Its bejeweled walls incrusted with emerald, topaz, jasper, amethyst, and many rare and precious jewels, sparkle and flash like the stars of the firmament. The streets of the city are paved with pure gold, clear as transparent glass. And yonder are the heavenly mansions, row on row—the trees of life, the flowing fountain, the pearly throne, surrounded by myriads of angels with golden harps that fill the balmy perfumed air with music. The light of God is on the walls, flooding the streets and tinting every spire and dome with a far more brilliant glory than the earthly sun.

And into all this glory, the saints are coming. Jesus Christ has gone to meet them. Descending with a shout, He has called unto Himself His living and resurrected bride. He is bringing this bridal body to present them to His Father without spot and without wrinkle. How they are singing—singing of Jesus and His precious blood through which they overcame! Shouts and songs and glad "Hosannas" make the heavens tremble as they near the beautiful gates.

Blessed, happy, honored people, they were true in the midst of test and tribulation—now they shall sit upon the throne and reign with Jesus. Faithfully they bore the cross—now they shall wear the crown. Ever believing, nothing doubting; though the night was dark, the valley deep, and the pathway rugged, they were led by a faith that never wavered even though it could not see or understand, a faith that whispered, "Faint not, fear not, but believe; though now, through the mist that hangs between, you see darkly but through a glass, you shall soon see face-to-face. The Sun of Righteousness shall soon arise with healing in His wings. Then shall shades of night and the gathered mist be rolled away."

And now here they are! John sees them coming in their robes of dazzling white, sees them stand—"*A great multitude, which no man could number…stood before the throne, and before the Lamb, clothed with white robes*" (Revelation 7:9)—and hears them cry with a loud voice, "*Salvation to our God which sitteth upon the throne and unto the Lamb*" (verse 10) and, "*Blessing, and honour, and glory, and power, be unto him that sitteth upon the throne, and unto the Lamb for ever and ever*" (Revelation 5:13)."

They shout till the sound is as the rolling of thunderous breakers on a thousand shores. Tears are over; sorrow is over; poverty, death, misunderstanding—all, all are over! Christ has come, and He has said, "Well done."

Glory! Glory! Glory to Jesus! What a vision. What a hope! Why, it dims our eyes with tears and melts our hearts with adoration and with longing, that we, too, may be a member of that bridal body when the saints go sweeping in.

Oh, that we may be ready—*ready*, did I say? Ah, how much that little word means! How it sobers our hearts and sends us flying to our Bibles and our knees, crying, "Jesus, search me; Jesus, fill me; use me; make me just what You would have me to be, that I may be ready, steadfast, immovable, waiting for the coming of the Lord."

Ready! How solemnly Christ inscribed the Word in burning letters all along the path of life. "*Be ye also ready: for in such an hour as ye think not the Son of man cometh*" (Matthew 24:44). *Ready!* Why, the greatest calamity that could befall mankind would be that of being found unprepared when Jesus swings heaven's portals wide and comes to claim His own. We know full well that the Bridegroom is not coming for a cold, backslidden, worldly bride— a church whose garments are besmirched with earthly pride and sin and merry making—whose heart is cold, whose eyes hang low with slumber, whose lamps have gone out for want of oil, and upon whose altars the fires of holy love and praise and zeal have died, leaving but the ashes of dead forms and ceremonies.

He who once trod the sands of Palestine in His pure and seamless robe is purer than the lilies and fairer than the dawn; holy, loving, sinless, true, He will call unto Himself a bride whose adoration and tireless running after this the Christ have wrought a marvelous transformation in her life. His own attributes have been wrought in her. His loving tenderness of souls; His patience and forgiveness; His calm, sweet, powerful Word—all have now become a part of her. For by His spirit and her obedient love, she has been transformed into His own image. Clad in pure garments of righteousness, whose fine needlework is wrought in gold of Ophir, she shall be brought unto the King and reign by His side in everlasting joy.

Once, the overcomers who compose this bridal body were sinners, unlovely, and far from God; now they are saints of the Most High. Many members, from many lands and climates, are made one in Christ, "*baptized into one body*" (1 Corinthians 12:13).

They are awakened virgins, whose vessels are filled with the oil of the Holy Spirit and whose brightly burning lamps are as a city set upon a hill, dispelling the darkness, lighting the gloom, and guiding the wanderer home.

These are they who "*love his appearing*" (2 Timothy 4:8), whose ready, waiting hearts have throbbed forth the soul cry of the blessed hope—"*Even so, come, Lord Jesus*" (Revelation 22:20)! They are the overcomers, whose feet have learned to walk triumphantly over the raging sea of life.

Roll high, you storm-swept billows of the sea! Rage and howl, you tempests of the deep. But over the heaving, ever-changing bosom, over the waves of daily tests and trials and tribulations that sweep the sea of life come God's fearless, trusting Peters. Their arms are outstretched toward Christ who walks to meet them from the distant heavenly shore. Their undimmed, luminous eyes, in which faith has lit a lamp and held it with a steady hand, are fixed on Jesus.

Through Christ, they are victorious. *In* Him, they are strong. *By* Him, they overcome. He is their all in all—Savior, Sanctifier, Healer, Pilot, Friend, and Lover. Soon, they look for His returning as the One who has the government on His shoulders, as heaven's Bridegroom, the eternal King.

Happy, happy people! What does it matter if the pathway leads over land or sea? If the journey over the waves is rough, know that on heaven's glassy sea, there reigns eternal calm. And O! that harbor is at hand! The Lord is near! What does it matter if the earthly path is strewn with thorns that pierce the feet and cause quick tears to spring unbidden to the eyes? Know that in yonder city bright, the streets are paved with gold. What does it matter if the nights be long and lonely and dark? Tomorrow's sun will never set; its light will never fade.

"Come!" says the Spirit. "Come!" says the bride. "Come!" cries the Word of God. Come whosoever will and join this happy throng who go with spotless robes and burning lamps to meet the coming King. They come by the way of Calvary, by way of the upper room, by way of a yielded, godly life, and tribulations' way. They are the overcomers, who "abided" day by day.

Oh, sleeping heart, awaken! Make haste, rise up, and shake the dust from your garments. Jesus is coming. In an hour such as you think not, He shall appear. Wash your robes in the blood of the Lamb. Receive the Holy Ghost. Then spend each waiting moment in winning other souls for Christ, that when He comes in the clouds of heaven, bringing all His angels to welcome you home, you may be found ready and waiting, bringing with you the precious jewels whom you have won for Him. Amen.

6

MY WONDERFUL VISION

It had been a hot and wearisome day at camp meeting. My duties had been long and strenuous. Now the last sermon had been preached, the last seeking soul faithfully prayed for, but I still knelt at the altar. The hour was so late, and I was so tired and empty. I felt I must ask the Lord to touch and bless me before I retired.

"Oh, Jesus, dear, precious Savior, will You please lay Your hand upon my head and bless even me? Let me see Your beautiful face, and hear Your tender voice; strengthen, encourage, and comfort me before I go."

Almost immediately, my prayer was answered. A sweet tranquility descended upon my spirit like a mantle from the skies, wrapping me in its holy stillness. How calm, rested, and detached from my surroundings I felt. My body slipped to the floor before the altar, but I made no move to prevent it, lest I disturb this "shut-in-ness" in the presence of the Lord. Then I saw a vision—

The whole world was wrapped in darkness. One could not see an arm's length through the blackness of the night. But hark! out of the gloom there came a sound of voices sweetly singing, "Oh, Lord Jesus, how long, how long before we shout the glad song? Christ returns—hallelujah! Hallelujah! Amen."

At the sound of that great "Amen," a streak of lightning tore through the heavens, from the east unto the west, dividing them in two. As I looked, the skies began to roll apart as smoothly as folding doors upon their hinges. Shafts of heavenly light came streaming down through the opening, piercing the gloom of earth and illuminating it with wondrous radiance. Through the aperture, I saw descending first the pierced feet, then the garments white as snow, then the extended hands, then the beautiful face and head of Jesus Christ, My Lord. He was surrounded by an innumerable company of angels. In fact, as quick as a flash of lightning, the entire heavens were filled with seraphic heavenly hosts—cherubim and seraphim, angels and archangels—surrounding the Christ of God. They were coming down, down, down in a beauty that begs description. I thought of those great sky rockets bursting in the air in multicolored glories and coming down in silent grandeur through the night. I know of nothing else with which to compare their wonderful descent.

Each angel carried a musical instrument. Many there had harps of various shapes and sizes. They were different from any that I have ever seen upon the earth and were of marvelous workmanship. There were those who carried long, silver trumpets and other musical instruments, the like of which I had never seen before. The first part of their glorious descent was made in silence. Then, suddenly, the Lord put His hand to His mouth and gave a shout, calling and awakening His people. At the sound of His voice, every angel struck his harp of gold and sounded upon the silver trumpets. (For years, people have talked about the lost chord, but oh, surely there has never been a chord of such melodious, wondrous beauty as this.) As they struck their harps, it seemed that the very stars of the morning broke forth into singing and trembled beneath its majesty. The earth began to vibrate, and the dead arose from their graves. They came from the East, the West, the North, and the South, and ascended through the air in beautiful white garments that seemed to float about them; their faces were turned upward, and their hands extended to the resplendent heavens. They were rising higher and higher into the air to meet the central figure of the Lord as He came down with His host of angels. As the resurrected dead rose through the air, they seemed to gather in toward the center of the heavens, taking their places as though they were prearranged in a shape that began to resemble a body.

Then the Lord gave a second shout, and, at the sound of His voice, the angels again swept their golden harps and sounded their instruments, holding the chord until the very stars shook, the earth rocked, and the mountains trembled. At the second shout, those who were living and remained upon the earth, whose garments were washed white and whose hearts were looking for the coming of the Lord, were caught up together with those resurrected from the graves to meet Him in the air. They came from every direction—from the mountains, valleys, plains, and the islands of the sea—to take their places in the body. Some were in the head, some in the shoulders, some in the arms, and some in the feet; for though there are many members, there is but one body (see 1 Corinthians 12.) What a picture! They were going up, and the Lord was coming down. Soon they would meet in the air, and what a meeting that would be! As I gazed upon this scene, I was overwhelmed, and my heart burst forth into the cry "Oh, dear Jesus, aren't You going to take me? Jesus, You know I love You; I have been waiting and looking for You so long. Oh, Jesus, surely You are not going to forget me. O Lord, take me!"

Suddenly, I found myself running up a steep and rugged hill as fast as my feet could take me. Once I stumbled and fell (that must have been the time I almost backslid and removed myself from the Lord's work, running from Ninevah to Tarshish), but I arose and started to run again. Up and up I ran, and this time, praise the Lord, I did not stumble. Up and up I went, until at last I had reached the top of the hill; but instead of going down the other side, I went right on up, hallelujah!

The bride was still rising to meet the Bridegroom, and I was rising, too. What a wonderful sensation—sweeping through the air! All weights and fetters laid aside—rising to meet the Lord. As I went up, however, I began to weep again, crying, "O Lord, is there no place for me in the body? It looks as though it's complete without me."

But as I drew near, I saw that there was a little place unfilled in the foot. I slipped in and fit there. Glory to Jesus! When the Lord gives us a vision, He does not tell us how high and important we will be, but shows us our place at His precious feet. It may be that the Lord will permit me to be a part of the foot of the glorious, running, soulwinning bride, until He shall appear to take us to Himself forevermore.

With the body completed, I seemed to be standing at a distance again. I saw the bride and Bridegroom meet. Her arms were extended up to Him; His arms reached out and clasped her to His bosom. Oh, that embrace! Oh, that meeting in the air! How can I describe it? The angels were playing softly now upon their harps. How wonderful the music was! They talk about Mendelssohn's "Wedding March," but oh, wait until you hear our wedding march at the meeting in the air. The bride, however, seemed to be listening to nothing but the voice of the Bridegroom. I saw Him wiping the tears from her eyes, and saying, "There shall be no more death, neither sorrow nor crying, neither shall there be any more pain; for the former things are passed away."

Now they were going up together—higher and higher they rose, melting through the starry floor of heaven, disappearing in the distance as the heavens rolled together again. Upon the earth there descended a deep, thick darkness—a hundred times blacker than it had been before. It was a famine for the Word of God. But up in heaven, a light was shining brighter than the noonday sun. Oh, how bright and glorious it was—the mellow, golden light of a newborn sunrise seemed to rest upon everything, tinting each spire and dome with a border of gold and crimson. Here all was life, music, and movement. The greatest day ever known in heaven or upon earth had dawned. The wedding day had come!

The angels had formed a great, long aisle leading from the heavenly gates to the throne of pearl, upon which sat One so wonderful, so dazzlingly glorious, that my eyes could not gaze upon Him. Line upon line, row upon row, tier upon tier—the angels stood or were suspended in midair at either side of the aisle thus formed. Above this aisle the little cherubim formed an arch singing sweetly and playing upon tiny harps.

As they played the wedding march, down the aisle came the bride and Bridegroom. She was leaning upon His arm and looking up into His face. Oh, the love, the joy, the hopes fulfilled that were written upon her fair and lovely countenance. It was as though she were saying, " Beautiful Bridegroom, Prince of Peace, Pearl of Great Price, Rose of Sharon, and Lily of the Valley—I love You, oh, I love You! How long I have been looking forward to this day; how I have yearned to see Your face, to hear Your voice. True, I have seen You darkly through a glass, but now, oh now, my Savior, slain Lamb of Calvary, I see You face-to-face! Oh, Jesus, to think that I shall live with You forever and forever! I will never leave You, but I shall lean upon Your arm, rest upon Your bosom, sit upon Your throne, and praise You while the endless ages roll."

As the bride looked into His face, Jesus, the Bridegroom, was looking down and smiling upon her, clad in white robes with her misty veil floating about her. Oh, that look in His eyes, that tender expression upon His face. 'Twas as though He were saying, "Oh, my love, my dove, my undefiled, you are fair. There is no spot on you. Before you loved Me, I loved you. Yea, I have loved you with an everlasting love. I loved you when you were deep in sin. I loved you when you were far away. I loved you enough to leave My Father's home to go forth to seek to save, to rescue, to draw you to Myself. I loved you so much that I died for you—I died to redeem you and to fill you with My Spirit. Oh, My bride, you have been faithful. Coming out of great tribulation, you have washed your robes and made them white in the blood of the Lamb. You have endured hardness as a good soldier, and now through Me, you are more than a conqueror. How long, how long I have waited for this day when you should be caught up unto my side.

"Often have your feet been pierced with thorns, but here the streets are paved with gold. Often the way was rugged and steep and your tears have flowed unbidden. But now, behold, the last enemy, even death, is conquered. Nevermore shall a shadow fall across your path nor a teardrop dim your eye. Forever and forever you shall dwell with Me in the presence of My Father and the holy angels, My bride, My wife forevermore."

As they made their way up the aisle and neared the throne, the angels broke forth into soft, sweet, singing:

Let us be glad and rejoice, and give honour to him: for the marriage of the Lamb is come, and his wife hath made herself ready. And to her was granted that she should be arrayed in fine linen, clean and white: for the fine linen is the righteousness of saints.   (Revelation 19:7–8)

As they walked into the brilliant light that sat upon the throne, my eyes were blinded by the glory, and the vision faded from my sight, but it is indelibly stamped upon my mind.

Oh, I am looking forward to His coming, His glorious coming, and the day wherein the bride shall be presented to the Bridegroom. Are you preparing for His coming? Would you be ready if even now the clouds roll apart and the heavens divide in two, and you hear Him descending with a shout? If not, come to His feet today, fall upon your knees in contrition before Him, and cry, "Oh, Lamb of God, I come. Help me to yield my life completely to You; make me all that You would have me to be; cleanse my heart; fill me with Your Spirit; fill my vessel with oil. Help me to bring others with me, that when You appear, I shall see You and be as You are."

Then rising from your feet with heart made pure and garments clean, your voice will be added to the swelling chorus: "Even so, come quickly, Lord Jesus, come quickly! Your bride is waiting and longing for You."

ABOUT THE AUTHOR

Aimee Semple McPherson (1890–1944) was a woman ahead of her time. She crossed the United States with two young children in an era when women were not permitted to vote. She established an evangelistic ministry and built a large evangelistic center at a time when women were expected to marry, have children, and leave religion and other "important" pursuits to men. But God had a plan for her life that did not take into account human ways of doing things. As an evangelist who preached the gospel not only across the United States but also around the world, "Sister Aimee" incorporated the cutting-edge communications media of her day, becoming a pioneer in broadcasting the gospel on the radio.

Upon opening the doors of Angelus Temple in Los Angeles in 1923, Sister Aimee developed an extensive social ministry, feeding more than 1.5 million people during the Great Depression. She summarized her message into four major points, which she called "the Foursquare Gospel": Jesus is the Savior; Jesus is the Healer; Jesus is the Baptizer, with the Holy Spirit; and Jesus is the soon-coming King. She founded the International Church of the Foursquare Gospel, also known as The Foursquare Church, which continues to spread the Foursquare Gospel throughout the world to this day. Recently, *Time* magazine named her as one of the most influential people of the twentieth century.